Queer Families

An LGBTQ+ True Stories Anthology

Edited by Curry & Sage Kalmus

Qommunicate Media

an imprint of Qommunity LLC

LANESBOROUGH, MA

Qommunity LLC
P.O. Box 454
Lanesborough, MA 01237
www.queerqommunity.com
www.qommunicatemedia.com

Publisher's Note: These Works are true accounts according to the Authors of the respective Works. The Publisher makes no claims of factual accuracy in these Works and the Authors take full responsibility for the content of their Work. In some cases, names and identifying facts have been changed to protect the privacy of individuals depicted. Copyright for each Work in this Collection is held by its respective Author.

Book Layout © 2017 BookDesignTemplates.com
Rainbow Interpolation on back cover by Matteo Niccoli, used with permission. Source: mycarta.wordpress.com.

Queer Families/Curry and Sage Kalmus, Eds. -- 1st ed.
ISBN 978-1-946952-06-6

Contents

NUCLEAR FAMILY

Gerard Sarnat

Anattā* (Haiku)

Queer, we're awed as kids
navigate among partner,
parent, child, non-roles.

*Non-self in Pali

Gerard Sarnat MD *has been nominated for Pushcarts. Gerry's authored* Homeless Chronicles: from Abraham to Burning Man *(2010),* Disputes, 17s, Melting The Ice King *(2016).* Kaddish for the Country *was selected for anti-Trump pamphlet distribution on Inauguration Day nationwide. "Amber Of Memory" was chosen for 50th Harvard reunion Dylan symposium. Sarnat's built/staffed homeless clinics, a Stanford professor/healthcare CEO, member of the longest-running Jewish-Palestinian dialogue group, served on New Israel Fund's international board.*

Spouses

Eila Algood

Weathering Life

It had been a hot August day on the Adirondack Lake, but the night turned frigid as the words on the television screen read "Princess Diana Dead". That's when the avalanche happened. Buried beneath emotions, I felt trapped inside a marriage. Inspired to leave the comfort of my warm, home, I traveled to England and stood outside Buckingham Palace on a London Street with thousands of strangers surrounding me, watching the funeral cortege ride by. That's when blood began to circulate and oxygen reached my brain. It was a moment of clarity. Diana: dead at 36; I just 37. It could be me in that casket. I wanted more out of life. Not more cars, boats or stuff, but rather a deeper experience of life and of love. I wanted to be a role model of living my truth for my children.

Someone heard my plea, because one afternoon, as I looked into the rich blue eyes of a Norwegian woman, I fell. Not down into a dark hole in the ground, but into the deep, bright place of love inside my heart. Nothing prepared me for this excitingly beautiful, yet taboo experience.

Within the confines of my mind and being, I lived in ecstatic love. But like a freshly opened bottle of champagne, the effervescent love poured out. Once others could see my attraction, the snow began to fall.

My husband of sixteen years became sad which brought the first flurries. I placed my shovel on the ground and gently cleared it away. His sadness turned to anger and that made for a heavy slush, but with determination, I could still push it off to the side. But then it became rage; that was too much. I hid outside while he cooled down and the air warmed up enough to melt the frozen mass of fury.

I came inside for a much needed break, but there's no rest for the weary as a knock upon the door called me. "You've been served" is what the man said. The blizzard began as lies and twisted truths were scattered on the divorce documents. I thought, "I must keep my path clear" so I began to shovel quickly and methodically. The forecast wasn't favorable. The sub zero air tested my strength when I heard about the private detective who'd been following me. Feeling terrorized and unsafe, I accessed courage and continued moving forward. I found a new home that was warm and safe.

The last few flakes glided back and forth like a pendulum in the night sky. As I walked into the quiet, empty house, which I now called home, tears streamed down my face. Feeling forlorn, I called out to my deceased ancestors: "Mom, Grandma, Auntie's, are you there? Help me be strong and to live from love, not succumb to fear. I can do this with your support." A wave of warmth entered my heart and I knew they were present as I fell into a deep, peaceful sleep. Their love empowered me to clear the snowy trail.

In the light of day, I breathed in joy from the cool air, unaware of the tragedy about to unfold. As I gazed into the eyes of my new love, I noticed a gray haze clouding their cobalt blue hue. Hail balls of cancer began to descend. I laid the shovel aside to be with her in the warm house. We cuddled together on the couch, sipping herbal tea. We learned that life was a gift and we had that moment. Holding hands, I infused love into her. Together, we plowed through the accumulated cancer.

On a cheerful bright and sunny day, the oncologist stated the morning sky was azure blue and cancer free. No snow, no sadness; we danced in the love together, flying through rainbows and walking on red rocks. We rode the bright sunrays over the sea to Norway, laughing and loving with family.

Joyfulness waned as storm clouds increased and a snow squall appeared. The dancing ceased. I picked up the shovel as frozen pellets of cancer began to cover the path, again. But I recognized it was her path they were on, not mine. With love and sorrow, I assisted her in clearing the way until it was time for her to go.

Upon her death, I noticed deep white snow surrounded me. Overcome with exhaustion I lay down on my back. Weepy water flowed from my cold, sad face. Submerged in the freezing wet snow, feeling numb I heard my son's sweet young voice call to me: "Mommy, I miss you". He was barely audible. "Mommy, come home." I had to get up and shovel, no matter how exhausted I felt because my children needed me, and I, them.

Although it felt impossible for me to stand up, I dug deep within myself for the energy to place the shovel down and push through my grief- and pain-filled heart while imagining their illuminated faces at the end of the path.

My daughter's smile and my son's eyes embraced me like a warm woolen blanket. Their love began to defrost the icy tundra that surrounded my broken heart. We cuddled on the couch. Their warm smiles melted my sadness as love replaced ice.

As winter ended and springtime blossomed, a new romance found it's way to my doorstep.

Gentle love rained down soft, warm water droplets, and completely melted my chilled heart; dripping gentleness into the caverns and tenderness into the cracks; restoring the wounded cells to wholeness. My brown eyed love and I embraced our lives together. Creating a surname to share and flying off to Canada where it was legal for two women to wed, we left our past. Although there were more snow squalls, we weathered them together, pushing through with our supersonic snow blower. Years later when the snow melted, we moved on to embrace the tropical paradise of our lives, where windy blue skies and iridescent rainbows abound.

Eila Algood: A native New Yorker living her dream life in Hawai'i with wife, Holly, Eila has been writing since childhood with published works: On The Road To Bliss, Rhapsody in Bohemia, *and pieces in* Frida Magazine *and* Think Pink Anthology. *As deejay of* Women's Voices *on KNKR radio she plays song and spoken word by female artists. Speaking her written words in public readings is a favorite experience as it gives her the opportunity to share her positive, playful personality.*

Amy Lauren

Wake

Before my wife and I met, pastors snapped us
        like the spines of their Bibles.
Our bones thirsted from birth for milk
        but dried till they cleaved,
crescent moons in skies crying
        for starlight. Ghosts
thrashed within our tendons and
        claimed our skin as their cells.

You ask of love in the wake of this,
        so I confess,
some nights, our skulls entomb
        and trap us
to nothing but trembles.

        Yet we still smile
when honey spreads on our chapped lips.
        We sprinkle water on surfacing
orchids and trace their emergent petals
        with most tender fingertips,
sitting side-by-side to taste the ocean salt
        without wishing to fling ourselves

into the coiling riptides of our pasts.

Which means that even these bones
still belong to ourselves, it means
we can sip from earth's fountains
and the scars at least keep it from all
spilling out.

Amy Lauren *is a graduate music student in Mississippi. Among other publications, her writing appears in* Sinister Wisdom, Wherewithal, *and* Lavender Review. *Her debut chapbook,* Prodigal, *received publication through Bottlecap Press in 2017.*

Rayna Momen

There's Someone I'd Like You to Meet

I remember when girlfriends
were roommates at family gatherings
deep in some hollow

like insignificant others, because
no one was ready to accept
that sometimes women love women

and we lived in Appalachia
where it takes a decade to catch up
to the rest of the map.

Introducing each other
we'd say friends instead of lovers
because we knew they couldn't handle
the topless mountains of thought

and on dates, people hoped
we were sisters, except
I was black and wild and you were
wonderful and white

and only our hands held the truth.

I'd wait months to tell my mother
there's someone I'd like you to meet

but it was better than some lie
and I had finally
run out of shame and fucks.

Today I am going on
three years of marriage
both of us from West Virginia

for once, not the last state
to do something right

though we still get
most everything wrong.

Rayna Momen *is an androgynous poet of color on the LGBTQ spectrum, born and raised in Morgantown, WV. Her work has appeared in several online and print literary journals, including* Skin to Skin, Wilde Magazine, *and* Cold Creek Review. *Momen is a W.E.B. Du Bois Fellow pursuing her Ph.D. in Sociology, and spends her time outside of academia writing and performing poetry as a means of challenging dominant ideologies.*

Rachel Walwood

Reciprocal, Shared.

I'm at the point in my life where conversations with casual friends frequently include a slow revelation of my childbearing intentions. I tiptoe around the topic in the same way I tiptoed around the topic of my sexuality with acquaintances in college. I signal and watch and if the evidence is satisfactory, I reveal myself as a prospective mother. Even though they hesitate, my friends almost always ask what they see as the two essential questions about how my wife and I will make a baby.

The answers boil down to: I'm planning to carry our first, and we'll use an anonymous donor.

Those two questions, from the outside, are sufficient landmarks to get from where we are—a couple with two uteruses and no semen-producing capacity—to the eventual end goal of a baby. From the inside, those answers were the easy parts of the journey. As queer people trying to have a baby, we know where we are and where we're trying to go, but we don't have a map. We're making our own way.

Even if it weren't for the fact that we're missing one of the types of gametes needed to make a baby, I know already that it will be difficult for me to get pregnant. I've been tracking my menstrual cycle since I was seventeen, and it swings wildly between poles of 24 and 90 days in length. The likelihood that I'm ovulating normally is almost nonexistent. The year we get married, my wife Amanda and I establish a loose timeline for when we'll start trying to get pregnant. With an end date in mind, I begin to ingest all of the information I can find about female fertility. My hope is that I'll be able to gain some insight that will help me shove my body in the right direction.

A year later, the podcasts and books I've been devouring lead me to self diagnose Polycystic Ovarian Syndrome (PCOS) and I start to delve into the world of infertility message boards. I hope to find a tribe, a community of people going through similar travails, to find advice and commiseration. Instead I find myself looking at a map that starts miles from where Amanda and I are. We're infertile and we haven't even started trying yet.

I read about straight women with PCOS trying to conceive and I long for the literal fountains of sperm they have in their homes. I wonder if they realize how lucky they are that they aren't paying a thousand dollars for the mistake if they get their ovulation date wrong. I boggle at women who say their husbands aren't willing to consider having a non-genetically-related child ever, no matter what.

I begin to mourn the fact that there's an unbridgeable chasm between my wife and I and the half-me-half-you baby that all of these infertile male-female couples are working towards. Then I feel ungrateful because we have the benefit of two uteruses and four ovaries. We won't have to pay a donor to get different eggs if mine turn out shitty, or hire a surrogate if my body is uninhabitable. And as I mentally play mix-and-match it occurs to me that I can have my wife's baby. Not in the pipe dream, "Why can't we make an embryo from two eggs yet?"[1] kind of way, but in a next year kind of way. In a her eggs/my uterus kind of way.

It's called Reciprocal IVF or maybe it's called Shared IVF or perhaps Co-IVF, but even if the medical establishment hasn't landed on an official term, it's a real thing that real couples have already done.

Childrearing and childbearing are an area of life where same sex couples face structural challenges, but we benefit from relative emotional liberation. When your relationship has two uteruses,

---

[1] "We Went to the Moon; Why Can't We Make A Baby from Two Eggs Yet?" Autostraddle. January 13, 2015. Accessed September 9, 2017.

there's no assumption that one or the other of you is more capable of being a mother. You begin asking Dan Savage's essential question: "What are you into?"[2]

I am into the idea of being pregnant. Of offering up my body and energy and my atomic matter to a tiny, swirling future-human that will grow, parasitic and symbiotic, inside of me. Amanda is into the idea of being a mother. Of nurturing a tiny person and giving them the experiences and knowledge and joy and passion she takes from life. She's also into passing on her genetics. She doesn't want to give up the opportunity to share the family history her genealogist father has painstakingly gathered, or to bring our child into the fold of her family that includes a yearly five-generations-deep reunion.

Most women don't have to make this choice, but they also don't get to make this choice. My friend Amy, who's pregnant as we're waiting to start trying, looks down at her seven-month bump and tells me "I'm excited to have a kid, but I would give up this pregnancy thing entirely if I could." It's a rare occasion that a woman in a

---

[2] Deitz, Bibi. "What's The Secret To Better Sex? It Lies In This Question Same-Sex Couples Always Ask Each Other." Bustle. April 3, 2015. Accessed September 9, 2017.

male-female couple gets to opt out of any element of biological motherhood. For the average woman, having a kid means getting pregnant with her own eggs and her own uterus. Period.

Over the course of the two days I look into Reciprocal IVF, it grows into a warm gem in my heart. I am in love with the idea of having my wife's baby. I am attached to the possibility of being able to say "we're both the real mom." I am excited to combine Amanda's genetics and my epigenetics[3], my wife's eyes and hands and knees and my blood and sweat and tears.

I'm not usually scared to bring my ideas to the light of day, but I fear that this is a time when I've let my enthusiasm convince me that of course we'll agree. I mention it tentatively over dinner by referencing a YouTube couple who documented their process of getting pregnant via Reciprocal IVF.

Amanda is open to the idea, but cautiously. It takes us twenty minutes of circular conversation to realize that she can't quite understand that I'm not attached to having a child genetically. In the same way, I can't quite understand that she's not attached to ever being pregnant.

---

[3] Lehmann-Haupt, Rachel. "Using Donor Eggs? Your Body Is Still Influencing Your Baby's Genes."

But the biggest stumbling block is logistics. Is this a path we can even take? I give her pricing I've pulled from our local clinic's website. We agree that it's a lot of money, but she says what I'm thinking: "If we have enough money to do it, it's more a question of whether having our kid this way is more important than whatever else we'd spend our money on. So, is it more important than, say, remodeling our bathroom?" We talk about it a little bit more, and I think we're on the same page—it's something we'd both like to do, but there are a lot of maybes. Amanda's afraid of the procedure, and we're both concerned about spending that much money on a gamble.

Over the following weeks we talk about it more. On more than one occasion Amanda says "I just think we should get a professional opinion. Would a doctor recommend Reciprocal IVF for us?"

She's looking for a signpost I'm pretty sure we'll never find. Based on my research, it seems pretty unlikely that any doctor will tell us to do IVF right out of the gates. Every doctor I've seen up to that point has told me that when I'm ready to get pregnant, it will be easy, despite my concerns.

But I'm seeing a new doctor now, trying to get to the root of my irregular cycles. My doctor runs me through the gamut of diagnostic testing. A few weeks later, her note in the online portal says: "Only one of your blood tests was abnormal, but that combined with your irregular cycles and the classic string of pearls cysts we saw on your ovaries supports the diagnosis of PCOS." I've been chasing a diagnosis for five years, and it comes as a relief.

In our follow-up appointment a month later, my doctor takes out a reproductive medicine journal and shows me an illustration of a polycystic ovary. There are dozens of circles inside the ovary. Each circle is a cyst. If it were a normal ovary, there'd be only a few circles and those circles would be follicles. At a certain point all but one of them stops developing, and that one contains a mature egg. She says, "The egg is floating in fluid in the follicle, and if we wanted, we could stick a needle in the follicle and suck the egg out. That's actually what they do with IVF. But for you we want to get that egg to ovulate on its own." She prescribes Metformin and outlines her plan to see if we can induce me to ovulate.

When I tell Amanda about my diagnosis and my doctor's assumption that we'll go with the turkey baster method of insemination, it surprises me that she seems to be boarding the Reciprocal IVF train instead. "We were always going to have to do it in an 'unnatural' way," she reasons, "Now we know we'll have to do it in an even more unnatural way. If we're 50% unnatural anyway because we're buying sperm, and then we're going to be another 20% unnatural because we're forcing your body to ovulate, maybe it does make sense to go 100% unnatural."

Our vision of our future child is coming into sharper focus. We agree that we are past the stage of just thinking about it. We both want to do it and now practical logistics are the thing standing in the way of deciding. What will it actually, bottom line, cost, and can we really truly afford it? Will we have to travel to do it at a more reasonable price, and can we manage that?

The next day, I get home from work and make a spreadsheet of six possible clinics. I scour websites and send a few emails and list out their prices for all of the aspects of the IVF process. I check flight costs and hotel prices and try to figure out how often we'd have to go out for the retrieval, how many times for the transfer. I check the statistics each clinic has submitted to the Society for Assisted Reproductive Technology (SART). Out of the options I've investigated, our local clinic has the highest success rate of the bunch, and is comparable with the other clinics for price.

Again, we discuss over dinner. It's the best outcome we could have hoped for from this particular spate of research. The clinic is three miles from our house, blocks from the birthing center I've had my heart set on for years. We agree that I'll call them the next day to make sure the costs on their website are what we'll end up paying.

Three days later, a full price sheet in hand for Reciprocal IVF, I make a spreadsheet that outlines our financial resources in comparison with the time we'll incur expenses, and what resources will become available at what times. I include when our car loan will be paid off, and the amount of money it will cost to give birth, and how much we need to cover our maternity leaves. I dive into our insurance documents and call our insurance provider to verify benefits.

I broadcast the spreadsheet onto our television from my cellphone and walk Amanda through it. We'll have to spend all of the money we can save up until we start IVF, and a significant chunk of the money we've saved over the past few years. But basically, we can afford it.

I ask a few friends why they save money if they're not saving it towards a specific thing. I'm hesitant to spend several years worth of nonspecific savings on something that feels in many ways like a spin of a wheel. Our clinic's high success rate still evens out to around 2/5ths failure. My friends largely say that they save so that when they have a big expense, they can cover it. Homebuying, career changes, emergencies, kids. We own a home. I just changed careers. Our emergency fund will remain untouched. We want kids.

Our appointment with our fertility specialist happens right as my clomid cycle is supposed to trigger my body to drop an egg into my fallopian tube. I pee on a stick three days before we go to the IVF clinic, and it tells me I'm having a surge of luteinizing hormone three days later than my OB suggested was ideal. The following day, my basal body temperature rises, suggesting that I've ovulated. The day after that, the day of our appointment, my basal body temperature drops, suggesting that in fact, no, I haven't ovulated at all.

That same day, we're seated in deep armchairs in front of a broad oak desk and our new, wide-faced, grey-haired doctor looks over my intake form and says "So your cycles aren't very regular."

"I'd actually say they're wildly irregular," I respond. He laughs.

He walks us through the process of a monitored, medicated intrauterine insemination (IUI) and gives us a fee sheet. He walks us through the process of Reciprocal IVF and gives us a fee sheet. Finally, we ask the question Amanda's been wanting to ask a doctor from the beginning: "Where would you recommend we start?"

"It depends on what you want to do." He says, gesturing his pen toward a diagram he's drawn of an ovary releasing its egg into a fallopian tube heading towards a payload of donor sperm. "Generally we start in the way that's the least invasive and expensive, so an unmonitored intrauterine insemination is where most people start. But then, if we inseminate Rachel, that's always going to be Rachel's genetics. If you want to use your genetics, we have to start with IVF."

And that's the essential question. Do we want to begin our family with a baby that is in many ways, essentially mine, or do we want to begin our family with a baby that is truly, biologically ours? I've read a lot of lesbian baby blogs, listened to a fair few lesbian baby podcasts and perused a bounty of lesbian baby Instagrams. I have heard couples state thoughtful intentions to parent equally as they're trying to conceive, and then seen them privilege the biological mom once there's a living, breathing child to contend with. I don't want our family's basic structure to defer to biology in moments of fragility or challenge, but I know better than to trust that it won't.

But we're still simultaneously plotting the path to IVF and the path to IUI, trying to decide which we can take, and which we want to take. I follow up with my OB to ask what to do now that Clomid has failed to make me ovulate and she sends me another prescription and a different timeline. I've been trying for two years to get my body to ovulate and it's not cooperating. I'm tired of trying and I don't even want to anymore. I don't want it to be my genetics. I want it to be Amanda's.

"I need you to decide." I tell Amanda. We're sitting at our dinner table, but everything else falls away from my memory of the moment. "I'm supposed to start my next round of Clomid whenever I get my period, and I don't want to do it if we're not even going to do IUI."

"What would you decide if it were up to you?"

"If it were only up to me, I'd want to do Reciprocal IVF. But I'm not the only one whose opinion counts." Amanda will be the one giving herself daily shots and receiving every-other-day ultrasounds for the two week treatment cycle. She'll be the one who will be anesthetized and whose ovaries will be jabbed with needles. It's her body that we'll be depending on to make this gamble worthwhile.

"How would you feel if you were the one making the decision on your own and we decided to do it and it didn't work?"

"I'd feel terrible, but I'd also be glad that we tried."

A moment. Chewing dinner, maybe, or contemplation. "When do you want me to decide by?"

"Next Sunday , maybe. Week after next, sometime."

She nods. Or maybe she assents. We talk about something else.

It's the longest I've gone for months without bringing it up. I go to work and do yoga and go on a run and pet our dog. I wait and wonder and worry and hope.

As we drive home from a camping trip to Lake Superior, I prod her again.

"I guess I think we should do it." She says. She's silent for a moment, the wind flowing between our kayak and the car buffering the air around us, a wide lake to the east. "It feels like we'd have to have a really good reason to decide that we shouldn't make a baby together, and I don't think there's a reason that's good enough."

We're still far from our destination. I know this, but suddenly it feels like we truly have a map, a plan, a peek at civilization.

I reach for her hand across the gearshift and hold it for miles.

Rachel Walwood is a computer programmer, knitter, and home-improvement enthusiast. She lives *in a century-old Minneapolis craftsman home with her wife Amanda and their adorable dog Willa. Rachel's queer theory research has been published in the* Grinnell College Academic Journal. *She identifies as bisexual.*

Parents

Chad Ratner

Being a Transgender Fost-Adopt Parent

I have a secret that I don't share too often. I am a transgender man. I transitioned from female to male 10 years ago. In those years I have grown into my new life as a husband and father. I have been married to a beautiful cis-gender woman, named Mel, for over four years. When we decided to have a child, we had several options to choose from. We decided on adoption, since I was adopted as a baby. While there are many different ways to adopt, we chose to fost-adopt; a process that starts as a foster situation and can end in adoption if the child is not able to be reunited with their birth family.

Mel and I knew it would be a long journey but decided that fost-adopt was the right path for us. When we started the certification process, I wondered how my being transgender might affect our chances of having a child placed with us. Should I disclose that I'm trans to the fost-adopt agency? If so, when was the right time? Would it automatically disqualify me as a fost-adopt parent? Were the social workers educated when it came to transgender parents or would they think I was some kind of pervert? I wasn't sure I should tell them I'm transgender. Although what if it came out later and became a problem that I had not disclosed this information? I decided to go through the process and if the occasion presented itself, I would disclose my secret.

We began the three months of required foster parenting classes, not sure what to expect. One particular class we were handed a form that asked some personal questions. One asked, "Are you and your partner able to have your own biological children? Explain." There it was. The place I had to disclose that I was trans. How would the agency perceive this information? There were several gay and lesbian couples in the class so I knew that there was no discrimination there, but what about against transgender people? We are a stigmatized community and I wasn't sure how my answer might be perceived. I decided that now was the time to come out. I wrote down that I was unable to have children because I was transgender. That was that. Someone would see my answer and decide if I could continue with the certification process.

As time passed, my wife and I finished the classes without the issue coming up. Next we completed CPR and First Aid training. Then was the fingerprinting and background check. Ah yes, another place my past would come up. I had to list my old name as an alias so that it did not trigger any red flags in my file. Luckily, no one said anything about my old female name.We also had to have a physical and a TB test.

Next came the home inspection to make sure that our apartment met all of the safety requirements. Mel did a great job preparing us for this. She purchased a fire extinguisher and a fire ladder. To baby-proof the place, she bought locks for all of the cabinets and even one for the toilet! We had the evacuation route posted. We had the "Foster Child's Rights" paper posted. Our medicines and cleaning products were locked up, as required. The number for poison control was posted all over the house. We were prepared and it showed. We passed the inspection!

The last step of the certification process was the home-study. We were both nervous about this part because it consisted of some extremely personal questions. Some of them were about our sex life, STD's, and pornography. Inevitably the subject came up that I was transgender. The social worker from our fost-adopt agency assured me that being trans was a nonissue! We were relieved to hear that I would be given an equal opportunity to adopt. At the end of the four-day study we were exhausted...but that was just the beginning.

A week later came the good news. We had been recommended as foster parents! Within days of signing our certification paperwork, a call came over my cell phone. I recognized the fost-adopt agency's number when it flashed on my screen and quickly answered the call. The social worker who conducted our home study was on the line with information about a newborn baby. The baby was born three days ago, addicted to drugs and was taken from the mother. The mother also had other children who were previously removed from her custody, therefore, it seemed to be a likely adoption situation. Mel and I had already discussed what would happen if we received this call. It was up to me to say yes or no. I made the decision to say yes to the placement, then called Mel excitedly to tell her we were getting a baby!

As soon as Mel got off from work we headed to the hospital. The baby had been detoxing in the NICU for the past three days and was now ready to be taken home. We met a county social worker at the hospital and all went up together to greet the baby. Mel and I had never seen anything so tiny. There was our baby boy. The biological mother had already named him Elias, so we decided to keep the name. As I held him in my arms

I felt a mixture of happiness and nervousness. We took him home, falling in love with him almost immediately.

I soon found that being a Dad was not easy! In the following weeks Elias would test the boundaries of my patience by crying all day and all night. He only slept in 20-30 minute intervals at night, and so did we. I was the primary stay at home parent as Mel worked during the week and I worked on the weekends. Often, I looked forward to the weekends so that I could have a little break while I was at work. We read several parenting books, hoping to find ways to soothe our baby. There were various techniques, such as: rocking, cuddling, whispering, shushing, swaddling, singing, and baby wearing. Some worked for Mel but for me it was harder to keep Elias from crying. I felt like breaking down most days from the lack of sleep. Elias cried if I tried to do the dishes or use the restroom without him. Taking a shower, injecting my testosterone treatments, and shaving my face, were luxuries I could only appreciate when Mel was home to comfort him.

I wondered what I'd gotten myself into and if I could handle it. I sacrificed my time for him every day and I was not used to being so selfless. Is this how my parents felt with me and my sisters? How did they do it? How would I do it? Thankfully I had help from Mel. I couldn't have survived without her. When she wore the baby in a wrap he seemed happy, often falling asleep right away. She read him bedtime stories, sang to him, enrolled him in music and gym classes, and nurtured him.

As the days passed, I got used to the routine of feeding, diapering, and nurturing our little bundle of joy. I learned which techniques worked best with Elias. We began swimming lessons and music classes. I became very attached to him.

I looked into his little eyes, thoughts of the future crept into my mind. I started to think about what would happen when it was time for me to tell our son that I was transgender. At what age should I initiate this discussion? Should I wait for him to initiate it? Should I disclose this at a very early age, such as during potty training? Should I wait until he is older so that he can fully understand what transgender means? Will his attitude towards me change when he finds out? Will he still love me? I think that the earlier I can tell him, the better.

I decided not to stress myself out about it. Since I often volunteered as a public speaker regarding gender identity, I was used to answering questions about my transition. I mostly spoke to college level Human Sexuality classes, so there were not too many questions I hadn't been asked before.

There were certain truths I wanted Elias to learn about transgender people. He should know that we are just like everyone else, except that our bodies didn't develop the same way as our brains. He should know that we are normal people that can have jobs, friends, and families. He should know that being different is okay. My volunteer work as a public speaker has helped to educate coming generations about gender identity. When the right time presented itself, I would be ready for Elias' questions. I promised myself to be open and honest with him.

We didn't really have a baby shower since Elias was a surprise when he arrived. However, when I told all of my co-workers that my wife and I were fostering a baby, they stepped up. I walked into work one day and found a box with my name on it. The box was full of diapers, baby wipes, and toys! What a wonderful surprise! Diapers were expensive and we needed all of the help we could get.

Mel's face lit up when I brought home the presents. I think she really missed not having a baby shower, so this made up for it! My wife and I soon realized some of the challenges that came with being foster parents. Luckily, my being transgender hadn't come up in any of this; primarily because I "passed" very well as a male.

There were weekly visits with our fost-adopt agency social worker and monthly visits with the county social worker. There was visitation with the biological parents for a few months, which was emotionally difficult for us, until they stopped showing up entirely. There were the assessment and findings meeting. There was Elias' attorney's investigator, who came to visit on occasion. There were many doctor's appointments; all were to be documented in our foster parent binder.

Finding a babysitter was difficult because they had to be CPR certified, fingerprinted, and have a current TB test. Every day there was something new we had to do, but we kept taking the necessary steps to keep our son. There were always court dates and then waiting to hear what came next. Custody was still being disputed. We were told it may take about a year to adopt Elias. This was one of our fears. What would happen if we raised Elias and then had to completely hand him over to his biological family? How would he deal with the trauma of losing his caregivers? He had already been wounded as a baby when he was separated from his birth mother. I couldn't fathom the idea of putting him through that again.

Mel and I hoped every day that we would get a call saying that the court had ruled in our favor; that we could legally adopt him. But time passed slowly. Often it was months in between hearings and we were not always privy to the findings right away. It was usually weeks later when we found out what happened in court and what the next steps were. Not knowing what was happening in court was stressful. There were two men named as potential fathers. One of the men was ruled out by DNA testing but still wanted to adopt Elias. The other potential father never showed up to take the paternity test, leaving us in emotional limbo.

Our agency's social worker did the best she could to get information about the case for us. Unfortunately, the county social worker was not as efficient as our social worker. The county social worker seldom returned phone calls or passed along any information. The only time we heard from her was at the end of the month when she was required to visit the baby in person.

The process seemed to be taking an unusual amount of time. Our fost-adopt agency advised us that it was in our best interest to hire an adoption attorney. They had reason to believe that we were being discriminated against.

Next came the county adoption worker who tried to ruin our lives. She found a problem with everything about us. She knew I was trans because she had read our home-study. She never said anything overtly to discriminate against me because, legally, she couldn't. The following day I received a surprise visit from her supervisor. She came to investigate our apartment because it had a "cat odor". Not wanting to lose our son, we moved to a new apartment within days. We even adopted out our cat.

Then things got worse. Right before Christmas, we received a letter in the mail from the county. It was a court order to remove Elias from our custody! This county worker really hated us. My wife and I were in shock. Mel took to her bed, crying for hours. I've never heard her make a sound like that before. She was howling like a wounded animal. I was sick to my stomach. I had raised and become very attached to Elias. We did not want to lose him.

We pulled ourselves together. We found it strange that the order to remove was dated weeks ago, however, it arrived on the last day that we were allowed to file an appeal. We quickly completed the paperwork, including a grievance form, and drove them directly to the county office before they closed.

After much anxious waiting for the next court session, the judge sided with us. Elias was not to be removed from our custody. Also, around the same time, the county stated that they "never received" the grievance we filed, which claimed we were being discriminated against on the basis of my gender identity.

The next time we went to court, the county adoption worker claimed that our fost-adopt agency was not an accredited agency. Our social worker was infuriated by this and quickly disproved the claim. The county was grasping for any reason they could find to take him from us.

What happened next was extremely upsetting. The judge would not yet grant termination of the biological parents' rights to begin the adoption process. Instead, the county attorney requested that my wife and I both get a psychological evaluation from a court appointed psychologist. The judge granted the request. We did not understand why. According to our attorney, the county wanted to determine if we were sexually abusing our son. There was no rational basis for this claim. We were being treated differently than other foster parents, simply because I was transgender. Since we had nothing to hide, we completed the evaluation. We were deeply offended, but what else could we do but comply?

Our next court date was postponed a few more months until the evaluations were completed. The psychologist didn't find any reason to suspect that we were sexually abusing our son. She completed her report but did not hand it to the court in time for our court date. We were to wait another few months for the next court date.

At this point, we were told that our county adoption worker had been taken off the case and we were assigned a new one. Several months passed with the new county worker, consisting of monthly visits with no updates, and no end in sight.

At our next court date, the judge finally terminated the birth parents' rights! Then we waited for the county to get the paperwork together.

We eventually received and signed adoption papers. After a few more months the county worker called us to see if we had received the papers back from our attorney yet. When we said no, our fost-adopt agency launched into action and discovered that the papers had never left the county office. Believe it or not, the county had "temporarily misplaced" our adoption paperwork.

It had been over two years that we've had our son and it took another month for the county to find our papers. They were forwarded to our fost-adopt agency, who forwarded them to our attorney, who sent them to us to sign and return. Not too long afterward, our attorney called and told us the final court date had been scheduled.

When adoption day came we were all ecstatic! Members from both our families came to see the finalization of our long journey. The judge banged the gavel for the last time and made us a forever family.

My mother and father-in-law threw a huge adoption party the following weekend. Friends, family, and even a social worker, came to help us celebrate Elias Phillip Ratner.

The fost-adopt process was long and painful. My wife and I were discriminated against by the county, for two years. It's a horrible feeling knowing that someone could just come into your house and take your child at any time. I worried every day that we would get unexpected visit and that the county would make up an excuse to take him from us. We both still jump every time there's a knock at the door. My wife and I have been through a lot. We have been told by countless people that we should sue the county for discrimination. We contemplated it, but decided that we had already been through enough.

To other transgender people who want to adopt children, I encourage you to do so; especially through the fost-adopt system. I'd just make sure to find a fost-adopt agency that will be on your side.

Chad Ratner is a transgender author who was recently published in the 2014 anthology, Manning Up: Transexual Men on Finding Brotherhood, Family & Themselves. *Chad has also served as a contributing writer for the magazine* Blade California *and has been featured on www.transgenderdaily.com. He received his B.A. from Queens University in Charlotte, North Carolina and currently resides in Southern California. In his free time, Chad volunteers as a speaker for PFLAG and is a proud husband and father.*

Todd Allen Smith

Bris for the Baby

When we got the call about our little bundle of joy, he was already born. Although we had been in the adoption process for a long time we thought we would have months to prepare once we matched with a birthmother. Instead there was a frantic trip to the store to get everything from bottles to wash clothes. There was also a bris to quickly plan.

What is a bris? Simply, it is a circumcision. Although not the basic circumcision I had in hospital, but rather there is a ritual and guests are invited to come and watch. Because we were adopting, there was no guarantee that our son would come to us uncircumcised, but we got lucky. You see we had agreed to raise our son Jewish and the bris is an important part of the journey for Jewish men.

So right after calling family, we went looking for a mohel. Who is a mohel you ask? He is a rabbi who is specially trained to conduct the bris. The mohel was an orthodox rabbi. This was important to my husband because he didn't want anyone to question the legitimacy of the circumcision, however it did represent a potential problem.

Orthodox Judaism is the one branch that does not perform or recognize gay marriage. So when he called, my husband made sure that the mohel knew that we were both a gay and also an interfaith couple. Interestingly, as we experienced when we got married, being an interfaith couple is at times a bigger issue than being gay.

While the mohel did agree to perform the ceremony, he let us know that our status as married interfaith gay couple wasn't an issue because he was performing the circumcision for our son and not us.

The only real question about the ceremony was how we were going to be listed on the certificate afterwards because it is basically a form that asks for mother and father. We let the mohel know that we wanted both our names.

After we found the mohel we made a list of who to come. First my husband's family was all asked if they wanted to attend. Unfortunately, only his father could come. Although his siblings would have liked to attend, they live far away and there wasn't time for them to schedule the trip. Traditionally, the bris is performed on the child's eighth day, and while we weren't able to do it that fast because we were adopting, we did it as soon as we could. Besides the short notice, our son was a hospital placement so we didn't know we were going to be dads until after he was born.

Then I had to ask to my parents if they were coming. They raised me Southern Baptist and are still active in their church. I also think this would be the first Jewish ceremony that they would attend, so it was a big question of whether they would come or not. I was ecstatic when they decided to attend. Because they weren't at the wedding, this would also be the first time my husband's father would meet my parents. So this was becoming quite the momentous affair.

The largest groups of people that were invited were our Jewish congregation and close friends. His birth mother was not able to attend, but our social worker from our adoption agency did come.

As part of the bris, our son was given a Hebrew name in addition to his English one. Traditionally, children are named after a loved one who has passed as a way of linking the generations. We named our son Andrew after my husband's great aunt Anna. She was a schoolteacher and her husband, who was a judge, never had children. David remembers staying at their house when he was little and the pears that grew in their backyard. While a child's Hebrew name is often similar to their English, we chose Moses. There were several reasons for this. First, using Moses allowed us to link our son to another family member, this time David's great uncle Morris. Morris was Anna's brother and never had children of his own. He was a pharmacist and we still have a bottle of Coca-Cola syrup (medicine, not soda) from his pharmacy.

Along with a ceremony, the event includes food. Which many times have bagels and lox, which ours did also. Yet, my husband also wanted to include other choices, such as his homemade banana bread, whitefish salad, fruit, egg salad, and kugel—a sweet pudding of noodles. He always makes too much. We chose to do the ceremony at our house, which many do, others might choose a synagogue or another event space.

The day of the bris was quite nerve-racking as we prepared the house for about 30 people to show up and have our son ready. The mohel provided us instructions to help prepare ourselves. Luckily, for everyone, Andrew slept well the night before and was in a good mood as we finished preparations. We then fed him about an hour before, which was what the mohel wanted us to do.

People began to show up about 20 minutes before the bris. Then the mohel came with a large case, the items he needed. I didn't look too closely; it was more than I wanted to know. We all gathered around the living room, where the ceremony was to take place. A chair, a table and our soft ottoman would be also part of the ceremony. Our child's Jewish grandfather would hold our child as part of the ceremony.

The ceremony went like this. First the baby was set in the chair of Elijah, our ottoman. Then he was placed in the lap of the Sandek, his grandfather, who held the baby during the circumcision. Then the mohel gave a blessing and the circumcision was performed.

Prior to the circumcision the mohel told the following story. During the time of Soviet oppression of Jews a couple wanted to have their baby circumcised through a bris. This was not allowed and if the Soviets even heard a whisper of a bris happening, the parents could be followed by the KGB for evermore. So the couple had to wait for the right time, always in fear they would be found out. After two months they were finally able to do it. After the circumcision, the mother passed out. They asked her why. She said she had fainted from relief. It had taken such a toll on her in worrying about whether they would be able to have the circumcision done before he was no longer a baby. It was an amazing story showing the importance of the tradition of the bris.

My husband and I also took part in the ceremony by providing our own blessing, which was sweet and nice and I enjoyed sharing in the tradition that went back over three thousand years.

As part of the ceremony, it is traditional for the baby to be wrapped in a tallis, a traditional prayer shawl. We used my husband's tallis, which was also used for one of his nephew's bris. Although our son's birth mother wasn't in attendance, we did include her by wrapping our son in a blanket that she gave him, in addition to the tallis.

As the mohel performed the circumcision there was an involuntary wince, which my husband later told me is another unspoken tradition shared by the men in attendance.

Mazel tov!

Todd Smith has over 20 years of writing experience. He has a Master's in Journalism from the University of Kansas. He spends his time raising his son and editing his book, Murder, Romance and Two Shooting, *based on his life and will be published by NineStar Press in February 2018. To learn more go to @toddsmithstl.*

Gail Marlene Schwartz

The Salad Spinner Chronicles

My formerly mellow two-year-old, Alexi, has recently turned into a maniacally obsessive student of domestic life. Considering his preoccupation with trains, I'm guessing his developing character is flexing its yin muscles in order to, however clumsily, attempt balance. I should be overjoyed but frankly I find it more than a little disturbing.

The first indication showed itself one day while I was baking muffins (wish I could say, "while I was repairing the leaky toilet," or, "while I was installing a new tiled backsplash," but that would be taking more than my fair share of artistic license). Alexi was rummaging through the one kitchen cabinet that we allow him to explore: home of Tupperware and all things plastic. I turned my back to grab the maple syrup when I heard a crash behind me. I turned to see the three distinct parts of our beloved salad spinner tumbling across the bathwater-gray kitchen floor. Then I heard a throaty cry bubble up from my boy's innards and explode from his gaping mouth. But it was clear from his facial expression that the noise expressed sheer delight, not distress. I looked at him, confused, and then picked up the plastic colander-like middle piece.

"THIS?" I said with disbelief, "This is what you want?"

He smiled, pointed, and said, "Babawawa."

Since he had never watched 20/20, I had to think more abstractly in my interpretation. So I put the three pieces together and placed boy and spinner in his gated play area to see what happened.

Pure joy ensued.

For months, the salad spinner fully occupied my son's leisure time. I marveled at how he never tired of pumping the spin mechanism, staring at the middle piece whizzing around, listening in awe to plastic hitting plastic, pushing the black button that stops the action and getting me or any other adult with a free finger to click the white button that locks the middle piece in place. Nothing, not a new-to-him drum, a Caillou plastic bath book, or even a bottle of soap bubbles with requisite pink plastic wand could woo him away from the big white gadget.

Nothing, that is, until he discovered something even cooler: the vacuum cleaner.

Our wonderful babysitter and helper, Marie-Ève, spends a few hours a week vacuuming the house. Maybe it's sleep deprivation, but I could swear she's been doing it the exact same way since Alexi came home from the hospital. Yet one day, the vacuum was part of the white noise of the household, and the next day, it was a baby Saab. I admit that my wife, Lucie, and I splurged a bit on this item, and perhaps there are adults who would find our yellow Miele efficient, or even, possibly, sleek. But to Alexi, discovering the Miele was like being born again (and thank goodness this time it did not involve my uterus).

Lucie, Marie-Ève, and I tried not to laugh at his expressions of ardor, and Marie-Ève even let him help push it across the living room on occasion. The problem came when the rugs were all clean and it was time for the Miele to go back into the front hall closet. Alexi, who in his 13 months had showed a prolonged and consistent attachment to just one toy, a stuffed jester called Petey, began howling as though a car door had closed on his finger. Trying to console him proved useless for a good 10 minutes. He was mourning.

Last week I had a daylong training in Vermont, the longest time period that Alexi and I have ever been separated. I called every night to see how things were going and to say hi to my kiddo. One night, when Lucie answered the phone, her accent seemed stronger.

"I drank half a glass of wine," she admitted. I asked her what happened, trying to stay calm.

"It was endless, just endless. First he fell on the sidewalk when we took the dog this morning and he got a big egg on his forehead. Of course it takes longer to recover from those things without you…"

"Without my breasts, you mean," I interrupted.

"Just after he stopped crying, he dropped Petey on the way home. Two seconds later, this Irish Setter came out of nowhere and grabbed Petey and ran. No more Petey."

"Oh no…not Petey!"

"Then we went to phone you and the cell phone was dead and I couldn't find the charger. At one point, he just finally had enough."

I continued breathing. Barely. "Then what happened?"

"I was trying to calm him down after his bath but he just kept crying and crying. So I went into the front hall closet to get the sling to strap him on me and rock him. I opened the closet door and before I even saw the sling, Alexi rushed in and threw his arms around the vacuum cleaner."

I bit my lips, crossed my legs, and prayed those kegel exercises had done their magic.

"He cuddled up to it and sighed. I didn't even bother with the sling. He stayed in the closet with the vacuum cleaner for 15 minutes. And then he did a little hiccup, took my hand, and up to bed we went. Like the whole day had been perfect."

Now, this new obsession may seem funny or cute, as it did to me initially, but quickly we realized it presented a serious logistical issue. Marie-Ève scheduled her vacuuming around Alexi's mid-morning and afternoon naps so as not to wake him. Now she had the added restriction of his presence because of his new relationship with the Miele. Every time she brings the vacuum out, she has to put it away. And putting it away in front of him spells trouble.

So we did what many 21st-century parents would do: we looked for a toy substitute. Incredibly, Lucie found one for $2 in perfect condition at Village Value, the local used everything store. It was brightly colored, toddler-sized, and had a noise that accurately mimicked the sucking mechanism. He loved it, played with it more often than the salad spinner, and he even gave it kisses when that loving feeling overwhelmed him.

But, unfortunately, he didn't break things off with the Miele. His obsession with the Real Deal continued and Lucie and I found ourselves speaking about the vacuum in code. We also started sneaking it out of the closet when one of us took him outside, and then, if we weren't finished vacuuming by the time he came back, we would hide it: behind doors, under my desk, and even once in the shower.

That got old, fast.

I decided to go with the flow, save energy, and build some arm strength: I brought out my old broom and dustpan.

But unfortunately, just this week, he started showing the same tendencies toward these more primitive tools. I tried to lure him away with his yellow Tonka bulldozer, his favorite book about caterpillars, or his riding toddler bus, to no avail. I try my best not to roll my eyes as he asks, yet again, to go get the blue broom and sweep the front porch or the sidewalk or Big Bear or our shoes.

I tell myself I should be happy that my boy is finding work associated with women so fascinating. I tell myself how great it is that he's learning these very practical skills and that he'll even be able to do some of these jobs himself soon. I tell myself this is an advantage of being a boy growing up with two lesbian moms: there is nobody to react negatively to these early passions. I tell myself that this kind of obsessiveness is necessary to become truly great at anything. And all of these things I know to be true. My problem is that I can't think of anything duller than those very domestic chores he's currently gaga over. I would rather spend the day watching a cement foundation get poured than repeatedly sweeping, vacuuming, or spinning salad. It's bad enough I have to do those chores myself as necessary adult tasks, but to do them ad nauseam with an edgy toddler is just not my idea of fun.

When I'm in a more pensive mood, I think perhaps our children bring us the gift of a fresh perspective, on, say, those daily activities we take for granted as tedious. Maybe I should change my approach to being frustrated or bored. Perhaps if I sat in the middle of the floor and explored the workings of my salad spinner on a bad day, I would not only feel better but I might possibly even evolve. And who knows? Maybe the mental, emotional, and spiritual benefits of spinning salad will be the topic of the next viral post on Facebook.

Gail Marlene Schwartz *was a semi-finalist in the* Tishman Review's *Tillie Olsen Short Story Award 2017, a finalist in the* Malahat Review's *Open Season Award 2014, fiction, and received an Honorable Mention from* Room Magazine, *2012, creative nonfiction. Her work has appeared in anthologies* How To Expect What You're Not Expecting

(TouchWood Editions, 2013) and Hidden Lives *(Brindle and Glass, 2012). This fall, an essay and a short story of hers will appear in Rebel Mountain Press' anthology,* LGBTQ2. *Her work has also been published in* Parents Canada, Room Magazine Online, Witty Bitches, Sunday@6, Poetica Magazine, *and* Wilde Magazine. *Gail sunlights as a copywriter (www.gailwrites.net) and lives in St-Armand, Quebec with her wife and son. www.gailmarleneschwartz.com.*

William Henderson

The Verbs of Mathematics

My children—Avery, in third grade already embarrassed to hold my hand in public, and Aurora, six and convinced that she is as much cat as she is girl—take turns telling me about their respective day in school, as I drive them home. The drive can take as few as six minutes, if I hit the lights at the right time, though this never happens. Ten minutes during which Avery and Aurora will talk, then talk louder, then talk even louder, words stumbling on top of words on top of their attempts to get my attention.

"We've been learning about the president and the White House where he lives," Aurora says. She adds, "We also learned about snakes and the differences between something with cold blood and something with warm blood."

The potential reasons behind the pairing of the two lessons—the president and cold-blooded creatures—is clearly lost on Aurora, though, if asked anything about the current president, says it's high time the country "dumped Trump." Avery says that Trump will be president for at least eight years, if not longer. He's convinced that Trump, of anyone, will find a way to amend the Constitution limiting presidents to serving no more than two consecutive terms. He's also nine, and, if pressed, could not tell you one fact about the Constitution, or Donald Trump, or even about why he'd rather contradict his sister than agree with her.

Their mother took an interest in politics only after Hillary Clinton lost to Donald Trump in the recent election. She posts to Facebook one reason every day why Trump is slowly running the country into the ground. She says she cried when the election was called for Trump, and in the weeks after, supported efforts to convince the electoral college to throw their support behind Hillary instead.

She and I share custody of our children. They spend half the week with her and half the week with me and my partner. She and I were married when the children were born, then I came out. Our divorce, though amicable, resulting in each of us losing 50 percent of time with our children. The children are always together. The days with them are loud; the days without them are silent. But this silence, albeit a silence I sometimes crave when I'm with them, is not always worth how empty the days without them can feel.

"Tell me one thing about animals with cold blood," I ask.

"Snakes are cold-blooded," Aurora says, "and you can't trust a snake."

"What else did you learn about snakes today?" I ask.

Aurora is stumped. She kicks the back of my seat, and I look at her through the rearview mirror.

"Rora doesn't know anything," Avery says. I wonder, sometimes, if he says what he thinks someone else is feeling rather than what he actually feels. Not that I feel like Aurora doesn't know anything, but I also believe that Avery doesn't feel that way either. But by saying it, Avery has my attention, which has, up until this point, been directed at Aurora and her six-year-old way of describing her day.

"Avery," I warn. "Be nice to your sister."

"Daddy, I love you," Aurora says, dodging my question the only way she knows how.

"Love you, too."

"See," Avery says.

"And what did you learn today?"

"Nothing," he says, which has become his default answer when I ask about school, not just about what he learned but about what he's reading and what he did in PE and even what instrument he played during music class. (Third graders get to pick each week between the recorder, the triangle, and the drums. He, more often than not, or so the music teacher mentioned at the school's Halloween festival, picks the drums.)

"You were in school for six hours, and you learned nothing," I say, though it sounds, even to me, more like a question than anything else. "I don't believe that you spent all day doing nothing."

"We did the same things we do every day," he says, as if that means anything at all.

I pull into the driveway of our home and turn off the engine. While I reach for my wallet and phone, Avery and Aurora unbuckle their seatbelts and get out of the car. They close their doors tight and wait for me to open the trunk so they can take out their backpacks.

"I'll close the trunk, daddy," Avery says, and, depending on my mood, sometimes I let him. But I don't let him today. He's not yet tall enough to really reach the top of the trunk, so he has to stand on the tips of his toes and reach as high as he can to *just* reach the top of the door to the trunk, and then, to pull it down, has to bounce on the tips of his toes to get enough momentum for it to lower enough for him to get a better grasp and then pull it shut. I don't let him today and he frowns. He walks toward the front door, where Aurora is waiting, and I shut the door to the trunk.

Moments like these I wonder if I should have just said yes and let him do what he wanted to do. Then the "what ifs" unspool: What if he closes his finger inside the trunk? What if he falls while bouncing on the tips of his toes, hits the trunk with his face, and knocks out a tooth? What if he somehow—and of course accidentally—scratches the car. These "what ifs" beads on a rosary chain of thoughts that wraps around my approach to parenting.

"I'll get the mail," Aurora says. She puts down her backpack, and climbs onto one of three chairs arranged on our front porch. The chair tips under her weight, and I move my hip and leg to brace the chair and keep it, and her, from falling. We learned that lesson the hard way last year, after which she had a bruise, and then a scab, on her chin for three weeks.

She reaches into the mailbox and pulls out a couple of magazines (O, Popular Science), the weekly mailer from Winn Dixie, and a notice from a mortgage company that is not my mortgage company promising me that by refinancing with them, I'll realize a significant savings each month on my mortgage payment.

I unlock the front door and push it open. She jumps off the chair (landing on her feet) and carries her backpack and mail into the house. Avery follows, carrying everything else. I go in last, closing and locking the door behind me.

Parenting is equal parts routine and adaptation. Aurora showers at night; Avery showers in the morning. They wake up at the same time, and while Aurora is getting dressed, Avery has breakfast (if he's hungry). After Aurora is dressed, she has breakfast (a chocolate-covered granola bar, usually), and so on. A routine that ends only after I've dropped them off at school, walking Aurora to the door of her classroom, and leaving Avery as close to the door of his classroom as he's willing to let me walk.

A routine that begins again when I pick them up after school, and is broken only by however much free time they get each afternoon—free time dependent on the homework they've been assigned.

Homework for a kindergartener goes something like this: Time how long you need to read aloud a handful of sight words (e.g. because, funny, great, learn); draw pictures to illustrate different types of weather and atmospheric conditions (e.g. sun, rain, wind, snow) and either read aloud from a book for at least 10 minutes or have a book read to you for at least 10 minutes. Aurora has long since stopped needing us to read to her. She's read through almost the entire Dr. Seuss library, our collection of picture books, and is convinced that she is ready for the Harry Potter series of books (despite her problems sounding out Dumbledore, Voldemort, and Dursley).

Aurora still feels like she's accomplished something when she finishes part of her homework. The tip of her tongue pressed between her lips, she draws pictures to represent weather or animals or the members of her family, and then she picks out a book from our library and sits at the desk in her room and reads, sometimes aloud but usually to herself. If she encounters a word she doesn't know, or can't sound out, she asks someone to translate, then returns to her book.

Homework for a third grader, or at least for my third grader, goes something like this: Packets go home Monday and are due back on Friday. These packets include worksheets for English, history/ social studies, and math. These worksheets cover concepts, if not topics, they've learned at some point during the year, but not necessarily about what they're learning that specific week. Third graders also must read for at least 150 minutes each week, and earn bonus points for reading more than that (but are rewarded only for reading up to 200 minutes each week; anything more, though encouraged, does not help raise their overall grade). Third graders are expected to complete the homework and the reading in between four and five hours, so an average of one hour a night of homework, plus time on the weekend to read.

Except that's not all a third grader is expected to do each week for homework. Avery also is given two worksheets of additional math practice (known, affectionately or not, as Sunshine Math). Students aren't required to complete the worksheets, though, students who do earn rewards (like an invitation to the school's end-of-the-year party).

One worksheet covers grade-level concepts:

The 6 fourth-grade classes at Marathon Elementary School are having a kick-ball tournament. Each class must play each other once in the tournament. How many kick-ball games must be scheduled.

Or:

Mark hid a $10 bill inside his favorite book. He forgot the pages where he hid it. If the sum of the pages where the bill is hidden is 177, on what pages will Mark find his money.

Another worksheet covers concepts they won't learn for at least three years, if not longer:

Imagine, an eight-year-old still mastering multiplication being asked to solve for x in an algebraic equation, and required to get the right answer or risk missing out on points necessary to "buy" their way into the school's end-of-the-year party.

Easy enough, when you're almost 40 (or, you know, in eighth grade, which is when I learned algebra), but not easy at all when you don't even understand what the question is asking you to do.

Simple, right? Show your child how to solve for x (or what the question wants the child to do). Except parents aren't allowed to actually teach their child how to answer the question. (Honor system and all; it's not like his teacher is at our house making sure that neither I nor my partner teach him how to answer the questions). Instead, parents are allowed to "encourage and facilitate problem solving; offer guidance toward certain strategies; and read aloud the problems (without emphasizing any key terms that may help them decipher what they're supposed to do."

We just can't give the answer (which, in the letter sent home at the start of the year, was more like: **DO NOT GIVE THE ANSWER**).

The verbs of mathematics, that's how Avery's teacher describes how children today learn. The verbs of mathematics: An *expression* is a phrase or sentence fragment, a question without an equal sign. (And its opposite, *equation*, is a complete sentence with an equal sign).

Equation
Ten is five less than a number
$10 = x - 5$
A number is less than five.
$x < 5$

Expression
A number less than five
x
Five less than a number
$x - 5$

We can't give Avery the right answers, or even hint at how to get the right answer. Either approach is against the rules, or so says Avery's teacher. Instead, we're allowed to read aloud the question, sometimes emphasizing a specific part of the question that should—but may not—help Avery figure out how to solve the question (and, hopefully, reach the right answer).

So homework in third grade, or at least for my third grader, lasts much longer than an hour a night, mostly because my partner and I carry the responsibility of helping him finish his homework.

An equation of divorce:

If Avery's fathers spend more time helping him complete his homework than Avery's mother does, and if Avery makes completing homework with his mother more difficult than he does when with his fathers, and if it's a week where Avery's fathers have only Monday and Tuesday night to help him complete his homework, then how much time must they spend on each night to make sure that Avery completes the entire packet, gets the right answers, and understands (and can explain) how he reached the right answer?

Three hours on Monday night and two hours on Tuesday night, it turns out.

Homework, then dinner—eaten at a reclaimed wood table that was refinished, re-stained, and placed front and center in a vintage furniture store on Central Avenue in St. Petersburg, Florida—then one or two television shows, then Aurora's baths, then bedtime. Between Aurora's bath and bedtime, Avery and Aurora brush and floss their teeth.

Some nights, when they whine about teeth time, I offer to let them skip it, but only if they're OK with waking up with rotten teeth. Avery, more often than not, is fine waking up with rotten teeth, but he knows I'd never *really* let him skip teeth time. Instead, he turns teeth time into an equation to solve: How much time is the right amount of time to spend on his teeth before my partner or I—

or sometimes both of us—ask him to floss and brush again? Four minutes seems to be around the right amount of time for a nine-year-old to spend on his teeth.

Aurora's only request during teeth time is having bubblegum flavored toothpaste. Of course, she's prone to pulling out 18 inches of floss to floss her teeth, and then "accidentally" leaving it on the side of the sink or even on the floor in front of the vanity. *An accident, daddy*, she'll say, and while I very much doubt that anything was accidental, I'll accept her explanation, if only to get her into bed as quickly as possible.

Bedtime stretched out like taffy stretches when pulled in opposite directions. Avery wants a cup of water; Aurora wants a story. Avery wants the light on in the hallway; Aurora wants the light off. And a cup of ice water. But not Avery's cup of water, because now he's had some of the water and she's too old to share water with her brother. And no bedtime is complete without a "squeezy hug," which is what Aurora calls hugs that take away her breath. Each request one step closer to when my partner and I can turn off the lights in the kitchen and dining room and share what little time together we can before it's time for us to go to bed as well.

Parenting, divided into small segments of time, and then into even smaller segments of time, until you no longer know any other way to measure time than as the time you're with your children and the time you're not with your children.

An expression: My children are not bullied because their father and step-father are together, and I worry that one day someone will bully them for it and they will resent me. An equation: Someone will bully one or more of my children because they have two dads, yet my partner and I will have taught them that what matters—the only thing that matters—is that they are loved and adored and have two fathers who don't mind spending hours each night helping them with homework (but not giving them the answers), picking up their dental floss, negotiating bedtime, and prying from them the details of their days.

This worry, another bead on that same rosary chain that wraps around my approach to parenting. Let Aurora get her ears pierced the week before she starts first grade. Let Avery have several boys over for a sleepover the night before he turns 10. Let them both watch movies with PG-13 ratings, explaining in vague terms what certain words mean (slutty was a recent one, which I said, and only because of the context, was another word for pretty but wasn't a very nice word and certainly should never be used at school or when they're with their mother).

Let them know the rules they must follow, the risk of consequence, and the benefit of knowing that growing up is as much their assignment as it is mine—an assignment with no easy answers and no simple way of solving for x. An expression and equation, a phrase and sentence fragment, a solution and a full stop.

William Henderson *is a St. Petersburg, Florida-based writer and father of two. He's served as editor of two newspapers (the Boston-based* In Newsweekly *and* The New England Blade*), contributed to* The Advocate, *and is included in several anthologies, including the recently published* SPLIT: true stories about the end of marriage and what happens next. *His memoir,* Second Person, Possessive, *was published in 2012. He received a Hearst Award, two New England PressAssociation Awards, and was nominated for a Pushcart Prize. He serves up slices of his life in 140 characters or less at @Avesdad.*

Joseph A. Shapiro

Family Dinner

I took an early train home from work that evening; anxious to do what I knew I must to get my new life underway. My emotions were helplessly tangled: anticipation and excitement about what lay before me; tremendous guilt for how I'd arrived here, and what I was about to leave in my wake.

I called Lisa from the train to tell her I was on my way home, and that I'd be there in time for dinner with her and the kids. To my relief, she seemed pleased. My children met me delightedly at the front door. "Well, look who decided to come to dinner!" said Marc, wearing his trademark goofy grin. At twelve, he'd reached that somewhat awkward tall and gangly stage. His head looked too large for his very thin frame, but his curly blond hair and bright blue eyes won people over in a second. Marc was always the charming one, and he could be very, very funny.

Emily, nine years old, gave me a tight hug. She had her mother's dark blond hair and my brown eyes. She wore jeans and a bright pink tee shirt—

pink was her favorite color. I could tell from her hug—and the look on her face—that she missed spending time with me. I hugged her back, and kissed the top of her head.

"Is that your father?" Lisa was calling from the kitchen. Thankfully, the spirited tone of her voice signaled an apparently good mood. At least for now.

"Well, if you guys don't let me further in, it will be hard to have dinner with you... and I'm starved."

"You're always starved. What else is new?" It was a classic Amy remark. She rolled her eyes toward the ceiling, a true Lisa trait if ever there was one. But that's one of the few things, besides her wavy blond hair, that my oldest child got from her mother: now fifteen, Amy was very much a chip off my block. Her interests were mostly creative—she loved to write, to sing, and to act. She was not at all athletic. She had always been emotionally dependent on her close relationship with me. And if anything gave me pause about coming out, it was my fear of the impact it might have on her.

My kids and I moved into the kitchen and took our customary places at the table. Lisa filled plates by the stove and brought them over one at a time.

The kids had no idea yet about what was happening in my life, other than what they could observe when I was home. "So Amy, what's going on in that big school of yours?"

"I've joined the Literary Journal," she replied. "The advisor really likes my poetry, but she said it's pretty dark." Only Amy could talk about dark poetry with an impish grin on her face. She was always one for drama, and it was sometimes difficult to discern whether her incredibly creative writing came from her heart, or from her well-honed ability to shock the reader with uber-emotional images, frequently related to death.

"I'm glad to hear your advisor knows talent when she sees it," I said. "I can't wait to see you published in your first issue."

Marc interrupted, "Yeah, and then you'll get called in to speak with her guidance counselor who'll want to know how long she's been this disturbed! Will you please pass the Coke?"

"Shut up, Cram!" I have no idea why Amy started calling him that. Now Marc and Emily were both laughing.

I looked around the table, trying to memorize the happy expressions on my children's faces. I was petrified for what the future might bring. How could I ever explain this exquisite pain to anyone else, if I couldn't understand it myself? I loved these kids more than anything or anyone else in the world. What was I about to do to them? How could I ever justify the damage I might do? But what if I didn't move forward? What if I continued to live a life that I knew was inauthentic at best, and who knows how disturbed? What kind of father would I become? How would they look back on their dad? And what kind of damage might that leave in its wake?

Lisa said, "OK, you two. Enough." These were her first words since we'd sat at the table. "Emily, tell your father what the coach asked you yesterday." Emily, even at her young age, had become quite a good soccer player on a recreational league soccer team. The girl who used to only wear dresses had become the athlete of the family.

Em grinned. "He asked if I would be a relief goalie when he needed one!"

"Wow," I responded. "Do you really want to do that? Isn't it dangerous?"

"Yes I do, and no it isn't," she said, flashing a bit of attitude. "The goalie wears a face mask and pads. I might tend goal on Saturday."

"I'll be there... but if there's a soccer ball coming at you, I can't promise that I won't cover my eyes!"

After dinner the kids adjourned to their rooms to start their homework, and I remained in the kitchen to help with the cleanup. I dove in before

I could lose my nerve. "There's something we need to discuss," I told Lisa.

"Can't we at least have one pleasant evening together without your talking about your gay stuff? Is that too much to ask?" Lisa's exasperation came on instantly. And the anger in her trembling voice was barely beneath its surface.

I bristled at her reference to "gay stuff," but was not going to let that deter me. "Actually it is. And this isn't about gay stuff, it's about my life. And yours."

Now her face was turning red as she glared at me. Her hands were shaking—never a good sign. But I continued.

"I know you hate when I walk in late at night, and to tell you the truth, that's not working for me either. I was honest with you when I told you I was going to start exploring what it means to be gay. And I am. But I can't spend an evening with a guy and tell him I'm leaving to catch the train home to my wife and kids. It just doesn't work."

"That's just too damn bad! Because you are a married man and you do have kids, in case you haven't noticed! It's about time you started think-ing more about them and less about your gayness!" Her voice was loud, shrill and shaking.

"Can we please discuss this quietly, before the three of them hear everything?"

"No, we can't!" Her anger was reaching new heights. "Is there anything else you want to tell me before I leave the room?"

"Yes," I said. My voice was quivering now. "On those evenings when I come home to be with you and the kids, I'll start coming home earlier, so that we can have dinner together, like tonight. I'll spend more time with them, and be around to help with their schoolwork."

"*What do you mean* 'on those evenings when you come home?'" She was screaming now. In response, my voice got softer, and I struggled to speak calmly despite the deep turmoil within me. "I've found a room in the city where I can spend a few nights a week. I'm going to start living life as a gay man. It will be better for the kids, because they won't be staying awake those evenings, waiting for me to get home."

"You will do no such thing!" Lisa shouted. With that, she took the plastic bottle of Coke from the kitchen table by its neck and flung it at the ceiling. It hit the white painted surface with a smack, and suddenly there was soda everywhere—on the ceiling, on the table below, and spilling all over the beige linoleum floor.

"What the hell is going on down there?" It was Amy, yelling down from the top of the stairs.

I rushed out of the kitchen into the front foyer. "Your mother and I are having a disagreement," I said, as I climbed up the first few stairs.

"Sounds like a big fight to me," Amy responded.

"Like a war!" Marc's head was sticking out from his bedroom door.

"Okay, you guys. Call it whatever you want. Just go into your rooms and get back to your homework. Okay? Let me work this out. Please?" I was pleading now. Trying to keep everything from falling apart at the seams.

I headed back to the war zone.

"Don't come near me, and don't think you'll spend our money renting some room," said Lisa as I walked through the kitchen door. "And now *you* can clean up the kitchen."

"Oh, that's just great. I'm so glad we were able to have this mature discussion." I couldn't restrain my sarcasm. As much as I should have anticipated and prepared for this reaction from her, I hadn't. And I resented it. I know I had no right to that resentment; but it's how I felt, and that's where the sarcasm came from.

Lisa stormed out, rushed upstairs and slammed our bedroom door.

The kitchen did indeed look like a war zone. Coke dripped from the table onto the floor; and dirty dishes, pots and pans cluttered the table, counters and stove. I tried to ignore the pounding in my head as I began to clean up the mess.

I slept on the couch in the family room that night, knowing that I'd have to get up, dressed and out of the house early, so I wouldn't have to provide any further explanation to the kids. When that happened, I wanted it to be in a planned and thoughtful manner. Not like this.

Joseph A. Shapiro was a fellow of the 2010 Lambda Literary Fellows, and is a graduate of the Hunter College M.F.A. program. His essay "Cellophane" was published in the 2016 anthology, Fashionably Late - Gay, Bi and Trans Men Who Came Out Later in Life, *Vinny Kinsella, Editor. It was previously published in the* Cactus Heart Literary Journal *(2014). He has participated in the* Tin House *and* Kenyon Review *writers workshops, and has recently taught Transgender Literature in the English Department at Hunter College. He lives in Los Gatos, CA, with his dog Oliver.*

Helena Lourdes Donato-Sapp

What is it like to be in a gay family?

What I like about having both a Daddy and a Papa is I get to do karate and theater and I like having ice cream at home.

People like me because I have two dads. I think this is because it makes me different.

They say nice things to me about having two dads.

What I have learned about being gay because I have two dads is that we have to stay away from some places in our area because there are people there who do not like gay people and brown people.

I also know that there are families of choice. That means picking your own family members. Like my Auntie Jill and Auntie Deb are my favorites aunties and I like playing with them and their dog Vera. I have a lot of gay uncles too. My gay uncles Jeff and Matt invite me to their house every Christmas

Eve and their dog Shlomo is actually my cousin.
Ms. Estrada, my kindergarten teacher, is my family
too.

Because I have two dads, I know not to shop at
Chick-fil-A because they don't like gay people. I
like their chicken so that is too bad. I have decided I don't like it anymore. I am looking for other
places to get my chicken.

I learned a long time ago that pink is for boys and
girls and blue is for girls and boys. And toys are
just toys and you can play with whatever you
want. I have a truck.

I am 8 years old and I know that feminism is when
you believe that girls are equal to boys. And I
know that misogyny is when boys don't like girls.

One of our family values is that we always love
homework. We also believe that everyone's body
is perfect just the way it is.

I have a white Daddy, a brown Papa, and I am
dark brown and it is kind of awkward and different
than how people think it is supposed to be. I think
it is different and sometimes it embarrasses me,

but when I am at home it is fun. I feel most safe at home with the three of us.

Helena Lourdes Donato-Sapp is 8 years old and is in the third grade. She lives in Long Beach, California in a little green house. She has a big aquarium and two birds named Apple and Sunshine. She is also an artist and one of her art pieces is in a curated collection in a museum in Chicago. It is titled "Mango" and is very pretty. Her Daddy is a teacher and her Papa sells houses. When she grows up, she wants to do kind things.

Children

Zoe Smith

To my Father

It seems like I'm always
Making the distinction between
'Father' and 'Dad'
For people.
I spent a lot of my time on playgrounds saying,
Everybody has a father
Not everyone has a dad.

I hate to be a stereotype
Ah, yes,
The black kid without a dad.
Everyone knows it,
No one mentions it.
Frankly, I don't mind being without a dad.
What I don't like is people thinking that
I'm missing something in my life.

I used to try to convince myself,
That I was better than other kids without a dad,
Because I still have two loving parents,
Two moms, by the way,

Queer Families

To all the kids asking
"Why do you have two moms?"
Like, "Why DON'T you have two moms, huh?"

But I've come to see
That having two loving parents
Does not make me better than a kid with one.
Having two moms does not make me better
Than a kid with a mom and dad.

I hate how people are only able to see their family
As the best.
They take their differences from others
And turn them into the norm.

I laugh when now, people learn that I have two
moms,
It's only then do people give me the go ahead,
Because, hey, "lesbians are hot", right?

One of my moms says that family
Doesn't come from only blood,
But relationships,
So I live in a family of friends.
And sometimes I get tired of people thinking
That my non-bio mom is any less than my birth
mom,
Or my "aunt" is any better than my aunt

So, To my Father,
Thank you for being the source of
All my sassy comebacks and mouthy recoveries

To my Father,
Although you aren't part of my family,
Thank you for making mine complete.

Zoe Smith-Holladay is a 13-year-old African American girl going into 8th grade at the Denver School of the Arts. She has two moms. Zoe has been published five different times, including in her school's literary magazine, Calling Upon Calliope, *and the black literary magazine,* African Voices. *She has a blog for animals, called* kidsanimalstation. *Zoe's work reflects her passion for both the arts and sciences.*

Andrew L. Huerta

God Bless June Allyson

My mother was diagnosed with Alzheimer's in 2014. She was already exhibiting signs of memory loss and having a lot of difficulty communicating months before her diagnosis. She would often be searching for words half way through a sentence and unable to think of the details she needed to complete her thought. While my family and I had brushed it off as, "Mom's just getting old", it all came to a head when I received a phone call from her one day. I had just left my office and was getting into my truck when Mom phoned me. She was frantic. When I asked what was wrong, she stated, "Andrew, everyone has left me. There's no one here. Where has everyone gone?"

"Dad is not with you?"

"There is some stranger in the house. I don't know who he is."

"Mom. I'll be there in two minutes. Do you feel unsafe?"

"No. I'll be fine. Just be careful. Please, be careful."

I raced to my parents' house only to find the two of them sitting in the kitchen. They were both crying. The moment I got there I knew that everything was about to change. My first thought was this was worse than I had initially imagined. My second thought was that my father was "busted" and I was witnessing something that he had been keeping from us for quite some time.

My father informed me of my mother's "episodes" where she would forget who he was, or would immediately get mad at him and claim that he was after her money or stealing everything from her. While my father remained calm and tried to explain everything as clearly as possible, I could see how upset he was. He looked exhausted and heartbroken, and I began to see him as my mother's constant caregiver. My mother on the other hand sat quietly and cried. She repeated how sorry she was, but I could tell that she did not fully comprehend everything that was going on.

The next week we went to see my mother's doctor. The good doctor used the words "dementia" and "Alzheimer's" interchangeably and inadvertently communicated to us that there was not much that could be done. Like a typical allopathic American doctor, he threw some medication at us and said that we can hope for the best. When we were done, my father went to go pay the copay, and my mother and I sat in the waiting room together. For the first time in months, I felt that my mother was truly present in the moment. She continued to cry and the reality of everything began to make sense to her.

"I don't want to be like this," she said.

I didn't know what to say to her. I knew the medication was not going to work; minimal improvements if anything. But I did know that in a few minutes, as soon as we left the doctor's office, she would forget everything and she would be calm and happy once again.

"Everything is going to be fine, Mom. You have five grown children, and everyone is going to step up and take care of you."

"Those people in my house," she said. "There aren't any other people in my house. It's all just me. In my head."

I sat there shocked at her immediate, improved level of comprehension. She was fully present and she could completely understand her own reality.

"Yeah, Mom," I said. "That's your mind playing tricks on you. All those men you see are just Dad."

"I don't want to be like this," she said again.

My father joined us in the waiting room and together we walked outside. In front of our doctor's office is a long cement bench and the three of us slumped outside and sat down there together.

My father cried and kept saying to Mom, "I'm so sorry." And my mother once again said, "I don't want to be like this."

The three of us, sitting on that bench together, just outside of the doctor's office, has to be the most surreal moment in my life thus far. The horror of my mother's diagnosis with Alzheimer's; the frustration of not knowing how to treat or handle the disease; the amazing way my mother was able to comprehend everything that was happening; the sadness in my father's reaction; and the beauty of being able to share such a pivotal moment with the two most important people in my life is something that will stay with me forever. But again, as we sat together and cried, my one thought was to just get her home. Help her feel safe again, in her living room, and she will completely forget about everything that has just happened. And within an hour she was home, sitting on her couch, relaxing, and telling me all about my brother and sisters, and her beautiful grandchildren.

My mother was born in West Bridgewater, Massachusetts in November of 1935. The daughter of William Shipman and Olive Lothrop, she was the youngest of three children and a self-proclaimed "spoiled brat". My mother always said she was the apple of her father's eye, and that my grandpa would do anything for her, all she had to do was ask. Whenever Mom would reminisce about her childhood, particularly of her younger years in Massachusetts, she always spoke of a time when she constantly danced in school shows or pageants as part of a small dance troop; skated every winter on what the locals referred to as "The Nip" or the frozen Lake Nippenicket; or used whatever nickels her father would slip into her pocket so that she could go see several movies a week.

But at the age of 13, everything changed for my mother. She and her family were uprooted due to her father's complications with asthma and moved across the country to Tucson, Arizona. Seems the dry, desert air was ideal for Grandpa's many respiratory problems, and they all moved into a single wide trailer in what used to be central Tucson. Mom began school at Tucson High and soon met the big man on campus. And yes, at a height of five-foot-two inches and 125 pounds, my father was one of the most popular students at Tucson High. Then by the age of 17, Mom was married, had her first child, and lived under the overbearing guidance of her new mother-in-law. And then by the age of 32, Mom had given birth to her sixth child and was a well versed and highly accomplished stay-at-home mom.

As the youngest of six children in the Huerta family, my childhood was dominated by my one older brother and four older sisters, and was more than ideal with a mother who could literally do anything. My mom could sew; she could cook and bake; she could cut and style hair; she could paint and draw; she could entertain and party with the best of them; and she could always hold her own when it came to trivia and anything having to do with pop culture. When I was 10 years old, my family took a trip to Los Angeles and I remember taking a tour bus through Beverly Hills where the driver pointed out the mansions of famous Hollywood stars, mainly from the 40s and 50s. And whenever the bus driver would make a mistake, match the wrong movie star to the wrong movie, or match the wrong movie-star-husband to the wrong movie-star-wife, my mother would chime in and correct him. So much so that by the end of our tour, the bus driver was calling her "Mama" and asking, "Is that right, Mama? Did Olivia de Havilland star in the movie, *The Letter*?" And of course my mother's response was, "No. That's not right. Bette Davis starred in *The Letter*, with Herbert Marshall. Olivia de Havilland starred in *The Heiress*, with Montgomery Clift."

I remember from then on becoming fascinated with old movies and movie stars, and my mother being the perfect teacher to share with me whatever she could about the movies she had come to love. I specifically remember, back when television only had four channels, PBS would sometimes show old movies and we'd watch *Auntie Mame* with Rosalind Russel or *The Unsinkable Molly Brown* with Debbie Reynolds. Or times when the student movie theater at the University would show *Gone with the Wind*, or *Spartacus*, or *Some Like It Hot*. And then, by the time we had bought our first VCR in the early 80s, Mom would share with me her true love of the great female stars of the movie musicals and we watched *Funny Girl* and *On a Clear Day You Can See Forever* with Barbra Streisand; or *On the Town* and *Three Little Words* with Vera-Ellen; and of course *The Easter Parade* and *A Star is Born* with Judy Garland. But I distinctly remember one day, when we were renting movies at one of the larger video stores in town, Mom pulled a VHS cassette out of their bargain bin. She was truly overjoyed with what she had found. She kept saying that it was one of her favorite movies when she'd started dating Dad, and that it had one of the best dance numbers ever filmed. Well, the musical was called *Good News* and the famous dance number was to the song called "Pass the Peace Pipe" which featured a large cast of dancers lead by Joan Mc-

Craken. But it was the star of the movie that stood out the most when I first watched the film; a young singer/dancer that I had never really seen before. That star was the young and incredibly talented, girl-next-door type, June Allyson.

As we sat and watched the movie together, I saw my mother light up when June Allyson came on screen, and I knew that I was watching something incredibly significant to her. Not only was this one of my mother's heroes, but it was also a woman my mother must have modeled herself after. I knew that when my mother married my father, she needed to become the prim and proper, incredibly well-rounded young blonde wife that her mother-in-law expected her to be; probably who everyone expected her to be; but mainly, a woman or an image that my mother wanted to emulate: the beautiful and charming girl-next-door. I know my mother saw herself in June Allyson, aspired to be her, and gained a great deal of confidence as she watched June Allyson movies throughout the 40s and 50s. And since that first viewing of *Good News* with my mother, I've also associated her with June Allyson. An idea that I kept stored away in the back of my mind for quite some time; kept there until my mother was diagnosed with Alzheimer's. When the disease began to take away certain aspects of Mom, I started to look for ways to stimulate her long-term-memory and find ways to help her remember who she was and what she loved. When we were alone together, I would try to bring up certain topics, listen to certain songs, or watch certain movies that would help her remember anything she could about her younger life, her life with me, and what she tried so hard to teach me about the things she loved. And the one thing that would always make her smile, make her ask, "Who's that?", or make her say "Oh... I love her," was anything having to do with June Allyson.

When the constant care of my mother became too much for my father, he finally asked his children for help. At the time, we were all sitting together at lunch and I immediately chimed in and said, "Mom needs time away from you, and you need time away from her. I can take Mom on Wednesday afternoons. I can figure out stuff that we can do together, and get her out of the house." My siblings agreed to help Dad with his house work, but I knew I wanted to focus on Mom. Give her a break. Stimulate her memory somehow, and let Dad have a respite. The Wednesday following our famous family luncheon, a brand new DVD version of *Good News* was delivered to my house and I slowly began to put together my routine with Mom. Remembering that my mother loved music by Barbra Streisand, Olivia Newton-John, and Neil Diamond, I created a "Mom" playlist on iTunes and began playing it for her every time she is in my truck. While she hums along to most of the songs and often remembers the words to a few of her favorites, when a June Allyson song comes on, she always stops and asks, "Who is that?" And with my mom's love for baked goods, before I bring her to my house, we stop at her favorite bakery, and spend way too much money on a dozen gourmet, fresh-baked cookies. The staff at the bakery have come to know us and our routine, and Mom loves the recognition. Then when we arrive at my house, my mother is greeted by two very friendly and ill-behaved dogs, who she has come to love very much, and she settles herself in my husband's large and extremely comfortable La-Z-Boy chair. Serving her her favorite beverage of diet ginger ale, we sit together, watch our movie musicals, and eat cookies. We often discuss the wardrobe of any female star who comes on screen, then sit for three or four minutes after the film, and review what we did and did not like about the movie. It was after our third June Allyson movie that I truly began to notice my mom's close association with the star. After watching *The Glenn Miller Story*, staring James Stewart and of course, June Allyson, Mom remembered how sad she was after seeing the film for the first time. She remembered how sad everyone in the movie theater was as she left. She remembered hearing the news when Glenn Miller had disappeared during World War II, and she remembered my father comforting her when she first saw June Allyson crying on screen.

Now after every movie, we practice our regular routine of reminiscing. When we get back into the truck, listen to the "Mom" playlist yet again, she remembers things about when she was young, she remembers things about when I was young, and by the time she gets home, she always remembers who my father is, that he is there waiting for her, and she always says how happy she is to see him again. That was the goal of me taking my mother on Wednesday afternoons. That was the hope of the respite that I could provide my father. That he could go do what he wanted to do. She could remember anything she could about her life before Alzheimer's. And that she would miss him and look forward to being with him again. While my mother loves old movie musicals, gourmet cookies, popular music from the 60s and 70s, and June Allyson, the one thing I know she loves more than anything else in her life is my father. And I have to say that the harshest thing I have seen while witnessing my mother's struggles with Alzheimer's is her forgetting who Dad is and seeing him as someone who is trying to cheat her. So giving the two of them a break from each other and helping her remember anything about who she used to be has also helped her to remember who my father is. That he is not several other men or some stranger in her house; he is the man she's been married to for the past 65 years and she always remembers that he is there waiting for her when I bring her home.

I have spent my lifetime stating that I have the perfect mother. A mother who provided me with a safe and stable childhood; taught me how to be inquisitive and self-sufficient; told me all the time that she was proud of me and loved me; and exposed me to the greatest female stars in the best movie musicals ever made. Everything I needed to know to not only live as a well-informed, out and proud gay man, but to also contribute to her continued care as she lives with Alzheimer's. Throughout all of this, I have come to appreciate what my mother has taught me. It is an education and knowledge base that has greatly assisted me in dealing with the changes that accompanied her diagnosis with Alzheimer's. In knowing and understanding the things that my mother truly loved, I can now easily engage her in activities that assist her in remembering herself. As we spend our

Wednesday afternoons together, she remembers herself as a wife; she remembers herself as a woman who often associated herself with June Allyson, the girl-next-door, the young pretty blonde with great determination; and she remembers herself as I will always remember her: as a mother who could do anything.

Andrew L. Huerta lives in Tucson, Arizona where he has spent the past 18 years in higher education teaching/advising students who are the first in their families to attend college. After completing his M.A. in Creative Writing and Ph.D. in Education, he is now looking to publish a collection of short stories entitled A Different Man, *and his first novel,* Raggedy Anthony. *His short stories have appeared in such publications as* Chelsea Station Magazine, The Round Up Writer's Zine: Pride Edition, Creating Iris, Jonathan, The Storyteller, *and the anthology* Queerly Loving. *His personal essay, "Divorce and Evolution: A Case Study of a 'Joto'" is included in the anthology,* Fashionably Late: Gay, Bi, and Trans Men Who Came Out Later in Life. *For more information please visit: www.andrewlhuerta.com.*

EXTENDED
FAMILY

Amy Lauren

Enough

If God is not
my wife's autistic brother
clapping at the choir's music on TV
and rocking back and forth,
nodding his head and humming,

and if God is not
his mother holding his hand in the car
during high traffic as trucks honk
while he whimpers in the copilot seat,
murmuring to him that she loves him,

and if God is not
my mother-in-law
who owns five businesses
but gives every penny to those with no home
and welcomes them into her own,

and if God is not
the homeless trans boy she invited to Christmas
who cut her lawn to thank her
and sits with her at church because

she still hates to sit alone,

then we got close enough.

Amy Lauren *is a graduate music student in Mississippi. Among other publications, her writing appears in Sinister Wisdom, Wherewithal, and Lavender Review. Her debut chapbook, Prodigal, received publication through Bottlecap Press in 2017.*

Aunts
&
Uncles

Sage Kalmus

"Uncle"

I'm an only child. Growing up, I used to begrudge my parents for not giving me a sibling. I resented that I would never be an uncle.

I once confessed this to my cousin, who's more like my sister, when we were young. She told me not to worry, swearing her children—the ones she would one day invariably bear—would know me as nothing but.

My cousin and I are the same age, just about. 7 months apart. I like to say we've known each other my whole life. She's my oldest friend.

My cousin has two real brothers of her own. I was always jealous of them because they had each other while I had no one.

She and I were always closer, though. We have more in common. We never really played with others like we were supposed to.

We tell people we were lucky to be born into the same family so we'd be sure to find each other.

We say we're blessed because we're blood kin and soul kin.

After her son and daughter were born I asked, "What difference does it really make if they call me, 'Uncle' when they've already got three real uncles of their own?" (because their father has a brother too). And that's not even counting all their second uncles, or uncles-once-removed, whichever it is. She said I was being ridiculous. "You're their real Uncle too!"

Incidentally, I understand that just because you have siblings, it doesn't mean they'll have kids. I do realize this.

I also understand that just because you're gay, it doesn't mean you won't have kids. Although I don't, and probably won't. Which means, if I ever did have a brother, hypothetically speaking, I might someday be an uncle, but he wouldn't.

I've never been good with kids. I hear that's common among only children. Evidently because we're selfish. We're used to being the center of everything. I always believed it's because I was never very good at being a kid. But maybe that's the same thing.

I was a sensitive kid. I cried a lot. Like a lot of little gay boys do. Except, I didn't know I was gay. I didn't know what gay was, except another word for wimp.

I had an Aunt Jean and Uncle Steve back then. I don't know how they were connected to our family, but it wasn't by blood or marriage. I only know that they were Aunt and Uncle, and I loved them the same. They lived in a Manhattan sky-rise with a doorman, which I thought was sophisticated. Looking back, I'll bet they knew I was gay. I wish they would have told me.

My parents are nobody's grandparents. But they don't seem to begrudge me that. I think it's because they agree I wouldn't make a very good parent.

Recently, my parents confessed to me that each of them, at different times, had wanted a second child. Just never at the same time.

My dad may not be anyone's granddad, but he's Uncle to the kids of all my cousins, while I am to only the two of just the one. And even to them, unlike me, he's the real deal. Because my cousin is his real niece. Our dads are brothers. Technically, this makes him their great uncle or grand uncle, whichever it is. (What? No second uncle or uncle-once-removed? What, no great cousin or grand cousin?) But if you ask me, he uncles like a regular grandpa.

He remembers their birthdays and holidays, takes them on daytrips, has them over for sleepovers. By contrast, I suppose I uncle more like a... cousin.

Sometime in his teens, my nephew realized that his "Uncle Sage" was actually his second cousin, or cousin-once-removed, whichever it is. He tried calling me, "Cousin Sage" once too, just to feel the taste on his tongue, I think. Or to test the waters. Either way, it was only once. His mother heard it too. And that was the end of that.

I told my cousin sometime soon after that her kids could call me whatever they want. "They most certainly cannot!" she said. "But I know they love me," I said. "It doesn't really matter to me what they call me." "It matters to me!" she said. And that was the end of that.

Incidentally, I finally looked up the difference between a second relation and a relation-once-removed. Apparently, there is none.

It was while living in Hawaii that I was first exposed to a culture in which all the children are raised to refer to all their elders as "Auntie" and "Uncle". I understand now that lots of cultures do this, that it may even be more the norm in the world than the exception, and that it was I who was late to this party.

In the gay culture, lots of older men form an uncle-nephew type of bond with younger men. Probably because so many young gay men lack older male role models related to them by blood.

My husband is an only child too. He says, "Only children should only be with other only children." Works for us.

My husband has no other family, outside of through me. And even when he did, they weren't much of a family.

This year, on the weekend before his birthday, we went to my cousin's boyfriend's place to celebrate. My cousin's kids, now 19 and 21, showed up too, to wish their Uncle Curry a Happy Birthday. We had so much fun that on his actual birthday a few days later, we returned, and again our niece and nephew dropped by to help us celebrate.

More recently, Nephew again experimented with dropping the "Uncle" appellation, this time not from my name but my husband's. Again, his mother put a quick end to that.

The next day, my husband called Cousin to tell her, just like I'd tried once before, that it was perfectly alright with him for her kids, now grown adults, to call him whatever they wanted. "It's not alright with me," she said. And that was the end of that.

Our niece is an insatiable explorer, ready to take a massive chomp out of this world. Our nephew is a boundless creator, inventing new worlds for us all to explore. But more likely they would describe themselves as misfits, geeks, nerds and freaks.

Just like their mother. Just like their uncles.

Sage Kalmus is the cofounder of Qommunity LLC and Senior Editor for Qommunicate Media, its publishing imprint, for which he edited Hashtag Queer: LGBTQ+ Creative Anthology, Volume 1. *His fiction has appeared in* Whisperings Magazine, Carnival Online Literary Journal, *and* Rose Red Review. *His essays and articles have appeared in* The Writer, The Hampshire Gazette, *and* Livestrong.com. *He wrote and directed three plays in San Francisco. He worked as an editorial intern for Dzanc Books. He is a three-time contest reader for* Salamander Magazine's *summer fiction contest. He's been a freelance writer, editor, and ghostwriter since 2004. He has a B.S. in Broadcasting and Film from Boston University and an M.F.A. in Creative Writing from Lesley University for which he now teaches writing magical realism. He lives in western Massachusetts with his fellow cofounder and loving husband, and their four-legged family.*

Nieces
&
Nephews

Richard Ballon

What we imagine and what will follow

There was a code in my house. Whatever you do, whatever you do, don't tell Aunt Mary. So in the years I did not tell, I wrote an imagined event called The Gay Who Stole Christmas, and recited the poem at readings and open mics. I would have the audience recite the chorus in a flurry of laughing voices, Whatever you do, whatever you do don't tell Aunt Mary.

After the poem you will discover what happened when I did finally tell my Aunt Mary.

***

The Gay Who Stole Christmas

I.

My parents' home smells of pork and mothballs, and corners brood with holy pictures. The top heavy Santa on the table

looks embarrassed by their stares.
Hundreds of knickknacks applaud
the pile of gifts about to devour the livingroom.

I try to wedge my coat
in a closet bursting with square dance petticoats
and jackets from the forties.
The telephone, foraged from some hotel,
blinks as it rings.
-Aunt Mary there? My lover asks.
-I'll be over in a half an hour.

II.

We have a Christmas Carol all our own.
One our neighbors have never heard us sing.
Whatever you do,
Whatever you do,
Don't tell Aunty Mary!

My Aunt Mary is the one
with a megaphone for a mouth.
In ten minutes
half of Yugoslavia would know.
My present relatives, you see,
who reside in villages east of Italy
think of my family
as a cross

between Dallas and Patty Duke.

III.

My lover looks at her.
-Is she that one?
Aunt Mary turns.
The lights on the Christmas tree
stop blinking.

-You're the one not to know,
he says, shaking her hand
and smiling.

My mother appears in the doorway.
The game of cards
in the dining room freezes
one hand hovering
over the unknown card.
My sister coughs.

-Not to know, she says

-What he got you for Christmas.

The card flips up.
My mother starts the vacuum cleaner.
My sister takes Aunt Mary by the arm

to show her pictures of Maine.
My brother-in-law let his smile
thaw.

-Make yourself at home,
my father says to my lover's back.

IV.

Christmas music blares
from the television set in the den.
The trombone section
sounds like Mardi Gras,
and my niece in her Christmas best
looks like she just stepped in
from Halloween.

At midnight Mass
I look at the pill box hat
covering Aunt Mary's hair.

-You have one just like it,
my lover says loud enough
to cause a couple to turn and stare.

The host fell from the priest's hand
and landed on the rug,
when returning from Communion

my lover took my hand,
and one of the holy pictures
in my parents' home
Saint Jude, saint of lost causes,
Laughed and laughed.

***

It had been a difficult year. My lover and I had split up six months after purchasing a house together. My parent's home was filled with the smell of lasagna and pork marinated in vinegar. Aunt Mary was in residence. I was showing her pictures of my home and in one of them stood my ex partner.

"And who's that?" she asked

"That's the man I bought the house with, but we split up after he started an affair three weeks after we bought the house," I said.

"So tell me," she said.

"Tell you?"

"Yes." She folded her hands neatly in her lap and waited.

"I'm gay, "I said, holding my breath.

"Oh honey," she said. "I've known that for years but didn't know if you were comfortable talking about it."

She kissed me and wished me a Merry Christmas.

Richard Ballon has been writing poetry and plays for thirty years. His plays and monologues have played in NYC, Boston, Chicago, Baltimore, Denver, Montreal, Toronto and London. His short films, Dear Edward, Benefit and The Pure Dark were selected for multiple festivals. His book: enough of a little, to know the all was published by Levellers Press in 2007. His monologue, "His name was Doug," was published in "Hashtag Queer: LGBTQ+ Creative Anthology, Vol. 1" by Qommunicate Media. Richard has an MFA in Playwriting/Screenwriting from Lesley University and is a member of the Dramatist Guild. More about him can be found at www.richardballon.com

Cousins

Michael Narkunski

A Private Person

With my dad, it was easy. At 14, I came home one night to find him watching a *Girls Gone Wild* commercial. In his relaxed, Israeli accent, he said, "Mikey, life is all about the *tzitzkes*." Without thought, I shot back, "Not for me, I'm gay," and went to bed. The next morning, we watched *The Ellen DeGeneres Show* together. "You know, she's gay too," he pointed out.

I knew Dad told Mom, despite their in-house separation, because she immediately stopped making her insidious comments like, "Oh, do you think that girl's cute?" and, "You'll never get a girl-friend wearing that!" But even though she was the one I made papier-mâché projects with, who took me to all my doctor visits as a sick kid—there wasn't one word on her end about my coming out, for years.

It was like a miserable game of freeze tag. Every time Bush and marriage equality was on the news, I froze. Every time *Will and Grace* was on, or I said something vaguely effeminate, I froze, just waiting for her to release me.

But this wasn't like my asthma or allergies, anything she could work to fix.

It was only while moving me into my college dorm, with every folded t-shirt feeling like a bitter goodbye, that I heard Mom sigh behind me. I watched intently as she forced out what I've been dying to hear... kind of.

"Do you want to tell me something about gayness... or not gayness?" she asked.

Or not gayness. She was giving me the chance to, please God, change my mind.

"What took you so long?" I asked back. But she blasted in her blunt Brooklyn manner, "I wasn't sure!" and "It is what it is!" Then she left, starting a completely new round of silence.

Cousin Sandy's death wasn't set to change much. It was during my first college break—Mom glued herself to SoapNet each night; I drank forbidden beer in my room with porn on a steady stream. In other words, I was only half-listening when the details came.

It was cancer. It was inevitable. She had no immediate family. She was too young. I had met Sandy a few times, so in some way I felt bad, but still rolled my eyes when Mom announced: "You must escort me to the cemetery. To be my rock."

I almost laughed too, but then remembered I had a new iPod I wanted to test out. My mother always called the music I liked "funeral tunes," so now was my time to shine.

The drive started awkwardly. The Flaming Lips didn't pop, The Arcade Fire was too on the nose. So, I eventually pulled out my secret weapon, "Evil" by Interpol.

"Sandy, why can't we look the other way?" the singer and I screamed, taking the deceased's name gleefully in vain. Then Mom's petite frame started shaking.

I stopped the song, worrying I went overboard this time. Her mouth opened and closed.

"The thing about Sandy was we all thought she was gay," Mom said.

Finally, I thought then, while pulling up my seat from recline.

Time to hear what you really think about me.

"Sandy and her business partner, Doris, were very close," she began, as I studied every movement, every tone. "And when Doris died, it actually didn't take long for Sandy to follow."

She straightened her back. *Either bracing for discomfort or proud of her storytelling,* I thought.

"I would have found out more while visiting Sandy's deathbed, but I kept being pulled out of the room by her caretaker—that bitch, Sheila."

OK, a villain. One who nurses cancer patients. Could mean anything.

"I asked Sheila about the couple, and she so-claimed it was all strictly professional between Sandy and Doris. But I think that was just an excuse, so she wouldn't have to bury Sandy with her —the same cemetery as my side of the family!"

Huh? OK, now it was made sense. Mom was finally fine discussing the taboo subject of "gayness" because she wanted my help figuring out a perceived secret plot, against *her*.

"Gaydar doesn't work on corpses," I said.

She shot me a glare; I turned away. I wasn't going to be used in a game of gossip like one of her soap operas. She basically went to Sandy's deathbed just to get the dirt on her sex life. Meanwhile, I wanted her to get the dirt on mine, to support me like when I was a child.

But it didn't matter. Mom just waited—and when we got to the cemetery—pounced. She was interrogating people before I had time to get my yarmulke on straight.

"We had our reasons," said one aunt, chin in the air.

"Oh, Sandy? Why she's buried here? *That's* a story," said another.

"Sandy was a *private person*," a cousin chirped in.

Mom wasn't satisfied. "These people are hiding something, I always know when someone's hiding something," she said, to my widening eyes.

Grabbing my arm, she beelined. I didn't understand where, until I saw: the only blonde at this heavily Semitic affair, the woman I knew to be the daughter of the alleged lover. As Mom led me through to this key witness, though, I slowly noticed that the figure wasn't hobnobbing like everyone else. She was sobbing—practically braying—while looking around utterly orphaned.

The kind of grief that pointed to only one final answer about Sandy.

Mom dove in to console her, strangely, the only one to do so, and soon enough I heard the wailing. "I know, I know, my mother isn't buried here! I have no idea why Sandy's being put in this place, without Mom, without anyone who meant anything to her. Why? Why?" But as Doris's daughter continued her plea, people turned away, pretending not to hear.

Suddenly, everything had to be re-contextualized in my brain: the euphemisms, the lack of feeling, the snickers.

That's when my face got hot.

It was on purpose, I realized. But not because of Mom. No, I was seeing firsthand the stakes of keeping your life a little too quiet. When you're gone, other people are in control. To twist, to shame, and to bury without a trace.

We gathered around the plot. Sheila, "that bitch," said her few words about Sandy's only love —for her pet dog. I clutched my Kaddish prayer card tightly, and looked over to my paling mother.

"Are you OK?" I asked.

She said it was just the cold and shook her head. Mom was still a mystery to me, yet this funeral was solved as the frustrating eulogy concluded Sandy, as once again, "a private person, with fine taste."

The rabbi asked, "Any more words?" and I wanted to scream out, "Lesbian, it's called lesbian! Dyke! Rug muncher! Human goddamn being!" But I was silent. So was everyone else.

This easily could have been me—a coffin as a final closet. "We all thought she was gay but she never admitted it," Mom had said. Meanwhile, I never admitted it all those years to my mom, waiting for her to speak. Underneath, I think I preferred it to be quiet if it wasn't going to be easy.

I was disgusted with everybody and myself and ready to get out of there as soon as possible. Unfortunately, Sheila rushed through the headstones after the ceremony, her clown-red curls bobbing. She stuck out her arms to give Mom a hug. I waited to endure their chatty, fake goodbye.

Oddly, though, as Aunt Sheila kept her arms out, I saw Mom just... stand there. Her face still didn't look well. I wondered if I should say something. Sheila did instead.

"Come on," she urged, "people are *watching*."

Mom looked around, to see they certainly were. Then she took a few beats, shook her head in disgust, and silently turned her back on Sheila and the whole affair.

Within moments, she was at the car, waiting for me.

I didn't move, taking a second to register what happened. Was Sheila the ringleader, trying to play nice with Mom, a loose end? What was her stake in erasing Sandy and Doris? Was it pure distaste? The travel business of Sandy's that she was apparently inheriting? *Did it matter?* Keeping this kind of thing quiet is an old story. I just knew I wanted to be behind my mom, and not even look back to see what must have been a priceless reaction.

After all, my duty was to escort her. To be her rock.

I got in the car and buckled my seatbelt. The ride home was quiet. There was no, "I did it for the gays" or "Now I'm joining PFLAG!" But it didn't matter. I know she saw the same thing I did in that cemetery. Maybe she even saw me in that coffin, too.

I sang Interpol's song again, this time with a bit more feeling.

"Sandy, why can't we just look the other way?"

I wasn't sure of the answer, but figured it was likely because so many other people did. And more than ten years later, still do.

Michael Narkunski *is working on his M.F.A. at Stony Brook University and holds a B.F.A. from NYU Tisch in Dramatic Writing. His personal essays have appeared in* Out, Narratively, Hippocampus Magazine, Full Grown People, *and* Off the Rocks Vol. 21, *an LGBT anthology. His plays have had readings and performances at Dixon Place, Nicu's Spoon, Players' Theatre, Naked Angels, and the Producers Club. "Noise", his Dogme-style short film, will have a NewFilmmakers NY screening at Anthology Film Archives. He grew up in Staten Island and made it out, for now.*

CHOSEN
FAMILY

Amy Cook

Morgan

Part One

December 5, 2006. It isn't yet brutally cold in New York.

I've just come out of a concert put on by the Youth Pride Chorus, a group I'd helped found in 2001. After years of attending rehearsals as an Associate Member of the NYC Gay Men's Chorus (my Dad sang as a Tenor 2), I'd been asked to spearhead the creation of a chorus for queer youth. At 26, now "aged out" of the group, going back to their concerts was a source of joy. On the sidewalk outside the concert hall, warm shrieks of congratulations rise and fill the night. The friends I'd gone to the concert with are mostly gone, but I hang back just to watch the kids enjoy their fans.

My phone buzzes against my waist. An email, time stamped 9:26 pm.

The subject line reads: *NYCGMC Membership: Nightingale Brigade Announcement - Morgan Rice is in the hospital.*

Cold, blue panic.

I officially joined the NYC Gay Men's Chorus in 1999, but my earliest memories date back further, to when my father would buy me a ticket for his concerts at Carnegie Hall. My father had come out later in life, and getting to spend time with him in the city, away from my suburban New Jersey normalcy, was wondrous. Morgan was one of the few men in the Chorus who was overtly welcoming of a frizzy-haired high schooler intruder at their concert after parties. "You must meet Barbie," my dad had said, referring to Morgan's drag persona, Barbie Stiletto. "Meet" quickly became befriend.

Morgan had a razor sharp wit, crafted over decades in the entertainment industry. He had been a volunteer buddy for Gay Men's Health Crisis, as far back as the mid-80s, helping people who could no longer leave their homes due to the epidemic that had besotted his whole community. Morgan was elected "Queen" of the Chorus in 1989, a sort of social chair, a role that he relished. Even a decade after his reign, he still organized parties for everyone who had ever been a Chorus royal. (When he invited me one year, because he thought it was important that I hold that piece of Chorus history for myself, I was floored.)

As quick as Morgan was to abdicate any sort of leadership (he once announced that he would sooner "eat dirt" than be elected a section representative), Morgan had a fierce protectiveness over his friends, and over the place in the world that he saw as rightfully his. During a retreat talent show one year, Morgan, as Barbie, famously dragged a painted wooden cactus he had found backstage behind the acts he felt were going poorly: a virtual gong. A stranger might have found it (and him) mean spirited, but Morgan was quietly eager to make people happy—even if it came at the expense of anything that was polite or proper.

Back on the sidewalk, staring at my cell phone, reading about Morgan's seizure, I yell goodbyes without explanation. It's 10:04, and I've got 56 minutes before visiting hours end to make it from 66th Street to 14th on the downtown train.

The subway ride feels interminable, packed with chatty folks leaving Lincoln Center and the Broadway theaters. They clutch folded Playbills in their hands. I wish to be one of them, going home.

I am practically heaving sweat in my puffy red coat when I arrive at St. Vincent's. The hospital, now shuttered, sat at the edge of the West Village, and had been the epicenter of heartache for so many gay men for the past two decades. As a 26-year-old activist with a gay father, I have long lived with that loss. It is not unfamiliar, but it is a blanket that is burdensome in its familiarity. It is wool, and scratchy and urgent.

"I'm here to see Morgan Rice," I basically shout.

After searching and searching, the desk clerk cannot find him,

She has a Donald Rice, but no Morgan.

And then I make a mistake. I call Mark, the head of our Nightingale Brigade to check. (Formed in the early years of the AIDS plague, the Nightingale Brigade was a group of men who ensured that every Chorus member, no matter how small their involvement, felt cared for in their time of need.) Mark confirms something I had known, and forgotten. Morgan goes by his middle name.

This, disastrously, trips some sort of hospital regulation. HIPAA privacy laws, of course, are put in place for the patient's protection. I've worked in the field of medical malpractice, and I completely understand this, intellectually. But it's now very close to 11:00, his middle name is RIGHT THERE, on the sheet in front of this faceless clerk, and I burst into tears. She does nothing.

I call Mark back.

Here's the thing about my people. They don't leave someone alone, and they don't give up in the face of failure. Mark quickly finds another Chorus member who is within walking distance of me. Of us. Ron, one of my favorite people in the world, and happily, a clinical psychologist, uses his medical credentials to fly past security, even though the witching hour of "no visitors" is upon us. Ron is a slight man with an enormous grin, the kind of person you meet and think, "This person must be a great hugger." And he absolutely is.

I wait for him. While I sit (on the floor, like an asshole), a woman in plain clothes walks in, and when the clerk asks for her ID, she says she works there.

"Don't you have your ID with you?" she is asked again. No hospital ID. No ID whatsoever.

Plain Clothes shakes her head. She is waved past anyway.

The clerk's next words burn and boil on my skin. "I wouldn't want to be a patient in this hospital. They let almost anyone up."

And I hate what I'm thinking now. Mostly about murder, but also, how if anything happens to Morgan overnight... how if I had checked my email five minutes earlier, I would have had Guy and Jacqueline and Jim and any other amount of people who love Morgan, who actually THINK before they speak, with me... how friends are the only family Morgan has.

I hate HIPAA laws. I HATE St. Vincent's. And I'm scared.

Another email goes out.

Please note - if you go and visit Morgan, please ask for the room of DONALD RICE. That is how they have him listed. If you say "Morgan" they will say they don't have anyone by that name registered.

Thank you.

Part Two
December 10, 2006

Rhe (Morgan's best friend) and I are talking in the hospital waiting room on Friday afternoon, and she asks me if I think that Morgan has lived his life to the fullest. I honestly can't think of anyone in the world who better fits that definition. Morgan was SO many things to so many people (and he kept his worlds rather compartmentalized... many of us around the hospital this week are meeting each other for the first time). People loved to be around him, and with him, and near him. He knew who and what he loved, and he guarded those things with his life. (I use past tense here because the present is fading.)

I don't know if I'm ever going to be able to talk about Morgan's death on Friday night. It feels too personal, to those of us who were in the room. I can talk about walking from St. Vincent's to the

Monster bar, and conning our way in without paying cover. I can talk about the absolutely disgusting first-ever martini that I had that night (Morgan's drink is a revolting thing called a Gibson... Someone should have captured the look on my face when they dropped an onion in my drink). I can talk about feeling December settle on my body as I slept, for the first time that week, for more than a few hours.

Part Three
December 23, 2006

A small group of us are cleaning out Morgan's apartment, so that the landlord can rent it out for a billion dollars. It is truly a magical place, with an outdoor terrace and the feel of a lovingly preserved palace. We're stripping it of Morgan's memory, and keeping that for ourselves.

I start with a bookshelf, boxing anything I think can be sold. I find a box with a huge pile of Polaroids, many of men who seemed to have had intimate relationships with Morgan. I wonder how many of them survived.

The first time I lost a friend to AIDS, I was 19. His name was Dickie Remley. Dickie was a mostly-internet friend who I'd spent a weekend with in Baltimore, at a convention surrounding a local production of the musical, *The Last Session*. At the time, I was a ball of aspirations and not much else. I was queer but not fully out, depressed, and directionless. But Dickie was a man who didn't have time to worry about how nuts his friends were. He accepted me wholeheartedly.

When he died some ten weeks later, I stopped functioning. Alone in a dorm room in Ohio, someone suggested that I read Paul Monette's *Borrowed Time*, a memoir about the loss of Monette's lover and dearest friend, Roger Horwitz. While my college friends I were going to parties called Philander's Phling, and planning their junior years abroad, I was holed up, learning how to survive. Monette's words seared into me, as I followed the story from a gay cancer in a headline to Monette wrapping himself in Roger's robe, after Roger's death, so that their dog, Puck, might again smell his master and feel whole. Over the next months, I would read everything Paul Monette ever wrote.

So, when, on Morgan's shelf, a copy of *Borrowed Time* appears, I am not at all surprised at Morgan's good taste or my good luck. To be comforted again by Monette's poetic prose! I turn the inside cover.

And there, scribbled on the first page, is the inscription:

Dear Morgan, I love you so much. Paul Monette.

"Put it in your bag," a voice behind me says.

I turn. My friend, Jim, who has for many years heard me pontificating about Monette's work, had seen this happen to me.

"Just put it in your bag."

Whether this book, signed, was worth any money, was meaningless. It was never going to leave my shelf again, aside from the times I've picked it up since to remember where I come from. I don't believe in fate or God or karma or anything, truly, but I believe in Morgan, then and still.

Part Four
October 6, 2006

I'm at a memorial service for Gary, a charter member of the Chorus who has died and left a husband and two small children. Jacqueline Jonée, a Chorus Queen, sits at the piano, purple gown and heels, and plays "I'll Be Seeing You". She begins her eulogy by mentioning that one of our friends wasn't well enough to attend, but that this person had guided what Jacqueline was going to say. "As everyone knows, darlings, for good advice..."

The congregation of us, maybe two hundred strong, chants back, "Call Morgan Rice."

Part Five
June 18, 2003

Carnegie Hall.

The Youth Pride Chorus is singing on stage for the first time ever, backed by the Gay Men's Chorus. There are less than 20 of us. Several members of our chorus are so closeted that they cannot put their real last names in the Playbill.

Because I am giving the introductory speech, I am waiting in the wings on the other side of the stage from where everyone else is to enter. Aside from the evening's showrunner, all of the members of the men's chorus, including my dad, are already on stage. I am shaking.

"You ready?" I hear behind me.

Morgan puts his hand on my shoulder.

It is a warm summer night.

Amy Cook is the Legal Administrative Manager of Lambda Legal, the oldest and largest national legal organization committed to achieving full recognition of the civil rights of lesbians, gay men, bisexuals, transgender people and people with HIV. She was a founding charter member of the Youth Pride Chorus, as well as a singing and associate member of the

New York City Gay Men's Chorus. She holds a B.A. in Political Science, summa cum laude, with Distinction, from Rider University. Outside of her professional work, Cook is an award winning lyricist (BMI Lehman Engel Musical Theatre Workshop, BMI Jerry Harrington Award for Outstanding Creative Achievement) and a multi-time marathoner. She is married to lyricist Patrick Cook.

ABOUT THE PUBLISHER

Qommunity LLC runs Qommunity: The Queer Social Network (queerqommunity.com & iOS/Android)—a one-stop media source, marketplace and social network for LGBTQ+ and allies, where diversity is celebrated and individuality finds sanctuary. Its publishing imprint, Qommunicate, launched June 2017 with *Hashtag Queer, Vol. 1.*

Sage and Curry Kalmus
Cofounders, Editors, Husbands

Also Available
wherever books are sold

Hashtag Queer
LGBTQ+
CREATIVE ANTHOLOGY
Vol. 1

40 Writers
Over 200 Pages
Fiction
Nonfiction
Poetry
Scripts
by & about
LGBTQ+

Edited by Sage Kalmus
Published by Qommunicate
an imprint of Qommunity LLC

ashtag Queer is a necessary and phenomenal collection of work by
array of talented LGBT writers. This collection creates a space for
riters to shine and entertains the reader while doing so. There is
something for everyone and readers will not be disappointed."
AMAZON REVIEWER

refreshing to have stories from varying perspectives in the LGBTQ
munity. I thoroughly enjoyed my reading of the anthology and was
rticularly impressed to see so many different formats presented.
Loved it."

**A safe and supportive space
to explore and express
who you are,
Qommunity is a one-stop
media source, marketplace,
and social network
for LGBTQ+ & straight allies.**

#FindFriends #ChatLive #ShareUpdates #JoinQlubs
#PostPhotos #WatchVideos #CreatePages #WriteBlo
#AttendEvents #SellStuff #BullyFree #13up #FreeSign